M000280096

DAILY PRAYER
AND PRAISE

VOLUME 2

DAILY PRAYER AND PRAISE

The BOOK *of* PSALMS
ARRANGED *for* PRIVATE
and FAMILY USE

Henry Law

VOLUME 2
Psalms 76–150

THE BANNER OF TRUTH TRUST

THE BANNER OF TRUTH TRUST
3 Murrayfield Road, Edinburgh EH12 6EL, UK
P.O. Box 621, Carlisle, Pennsylvania 17013, USA

*

First published by James Nisbet & Co. 1878
First Banner of Truth edition 2000

ISBN 0 85151 789 7 for the
two-volume set

Volume 2: 0 85151 788 9

*

Printed in Finland by
WS Bookwell

Cover Design: Mark Blackadder

THE PSALMS.

I.

PSALM LXXVI.

PROBABLY some illustrious victory was the occasion of
this ode. It especially celebrates God's glory in the
preservation of His Church. For this all praise is due.
Unto Him all service should be rendered. Exhortations call to be earnest in such exercise. May we
obey!

1, 2. " *In Judah is God known; His name is great in
Israel. In Salem also is His tabernacle, and His dwelling-place in Zion.*"

Beautiful for situation, the joy of the whole earth, was
Mount Zion. Its supereminent glory was the tabernacle, in which God's presence resided. This sanctuary
was the type of Christ. He is the revelation of God. He
testifies—" He that hath seen Me hath seen the Father."
It represents, too, God's people. In them the glories of
His name conspicuously shine. In them His perfec-
tions are revealed. They manifest Him as the God of

grace and goodness, whose love from everlasting is love
to everlasting. It is a grand word, "Unto the princi-
palities and powers in heavenly places is known by the
Church the manifold wisdom of God." In Christ is
God known. His name is great in His Church. May
His dwelling-place be in our hearts!

3. " *There brake He the arrows of the bow, the shield,
and the sword, and the battle.*"

Many foes at various times assailed the favoured
city. But God arose, and all their might was shivered.
Arrows might fly, shields might glitter, swords might
be brandished, and the battle might rage fiercely, but
all was vain when God protected. Thus, too, Satan
and all his legion use mighty weapons to destroy the
Church. Fiery darts fall terribly. Incessant warfare
rages. But God is a sure defence. No fatal wound is
given. His people are all safe. They are enwrapped
in victory.

4. " *Thou art more glorious and excellent than the
mountains of prey.*"

Zion is here extolled as grandly surpassing the moun-
tain-tops in which ravenous beasts mangle the prey.
So God's people, in whose hearts dwell the beauties of
celestial grace, exceed in excellence all wild and savage
powers who use their strength in cruelty and rapine.

5, 6. " *The stout-hearted are spoiled, they have slept
their sleep; and none of the men of might have found
their hands. At Thy rebuke, O God of Jacob, both the
chariot and horse are cast into a dead sleep.*"

The enemy may come on fearless in courage, stout
in resolve, but at God's word their prowess quickly
dwindles. In vain they look for conquest from their

own hands. Their arms hang down as broken reeds.
They may command the chariot and the horse, but the
God of Jacob speaks. The chariot and horse become
weak as sleeping impotency.

7, 8, 9. " *Thou, even Thou, art to be feared: and who
may stand in Thy sight when once Thou art angry?
Thou didst cause judgment to be heard from heaven: the
earth feared, and was still, when God arose to judgment,
to save all the meek of the earth.*"

Let us stand in awe of God. Who will not tremble
at His wrath? Who among earth's sons can stand
when His anger kindles? His eyes are on the madness
of His foes. He will arise to save His meek and lowly
servants. Then vengeance shall descend from heaven,
and the trembling earth shall cease its proud resistance.

10. " *Surely the wrath of man shall praise Thee: the
remainder of wrath shalt Thou restrain.*"

Man may rage, but God will use the raging hand.
Persecution enlarges the Church. The threatening
hurricane purifies the air. If wrath still lingers in the
heart, His curb will check it.

11, 12. " *Vow, and pay unto the Lord your God: let
all that be round about Him bring presents unto Him that
ought to be feared. He shall cut off the spirit of princes:
He is terrible to the kings of the earth.*"

Great is the Lord's glory in humbling the loftiest
potentates. Let us be wise, and vow allegiance to the
King of kings. Let us present unto Him, as a willing
offering, our bodies, souls, and spirits. He justly claims
all reverence. His service is the luxury of life.

II.

PSALM LXXVII. I—IO.

A TRAIN of sorrows moves along this page. Relief is found in drawing near to God, and meditating on His wondrous works. We may have like sufferings. May we find like rescue!

———————

1. "*I cried unto God with my voice, even unto God with my voice; and He gave ear unto me.*"

Before the Psalmist delineates his grievous state, he openly avows the action of his soul, and the remedy obtained. His voice was uplifted in earnest and repeated cries to God. He sowed good seed, and reaped success. Happy would be our case, if we converted sufferings into prayers, and made them gates of heaven. Let this be our resolve. It will turn darkness into light.

2, 3, 4. "*In the day of my trouble I sought the Lord; my sore ran in the night, and ceased not: my soul refused to be comforted. I remembered God, and was troubled: I complained, and my spirit was overwhelmed. Thou holdest mine eyes waking: I am so troubled that I cannot speak.*"

The days of the godly are often thus darkened. Troubles are needed, and therefore will be sent. But they excite the soul to seek after God. We have not a long road to travel. He always is by our side. The

Psalmist's present trouble seemed to be exceeding heavy. The spiritual pain gave anguish like wounds festering in the night. There was no respite. The usual topics of consolation failed. His case seemed to be hopeless. Even the thought of God brought not its wonted joy. Doubts cast a veil over His ready smiles. No sleep gave soothing ease. Utterance refused to be the outlet of distress. He watched in silence; and in mute anguish mourned.

5, 6. "*I have considered the days of old, the years of ancient times. I call to remembrance my song in the night: I commune with mine own heart; and my spirit made diligent search.*"

In meditation he pondered the records of God's ancient dealings. The annals abounded in evidence that God's love had never failed. They displayed His arm always mighty to deliver. He next reviewed his own eventful story. He remembered times of lively joy, when the night heard his songs of praise. It is well that like periods be treasured in our minds. Past pleasures should revive. He sought, too, the cause of his discomfort. He probed the recesses of his heart. He used all efforts to discover what leaks admitted these waters of bitterness.

7, 8, 9. "*Will the Lord cast off for ever? and will He be favourable no more? Is His mercy clean gone for ever? doth His promise fail for evermore? Hath God forgotten to be gracious? hath He in anger shut up His tender mercies?*"

Wave upon wave of doubts and fears break over the mind. Apprehensions in terrific forms appear like spectres. God's dark frown of anger seems to look

down. Smiles are obscured by unbroken gloom. The
gate of favour no longer opens. He trembles lest he
should be cast off for ever, and mercy no more give solace.
He plaintively inquires, Will lovingkindness no more
cheer me? He had feasted on the rich repast of precious promises; these promises no longer brought support. Can it be that he is for ever excluded from this
heritage of God's people? Grace is God's delight.
Can He forget this exercise of His goodness? Hath
anger so barred the door that tender mercies can have
no passage? Thus he questioned; and the questions
seemed to imply that such doubts must be groundless
temptations.

10. *"And I said, This is my infirmity: but I will
remember the years of the right hand of the Most High."*

Faith, though it had been downcast, revives. The
Psalmist sees that all this disconsolation sprang from
his own weakness. Spiritual power had failed. The
real cause was not in the wavering love of God, but in
decline of holy trust. He confesses, This is mine own
infirmity. He sees the remedy. He looks back to
God's dealings in the long history of His Church. Ages
have passed; but ages have brought no diminution in
God's power. His right hand, which had wrought
such wonders, is His right hand still, and never can
wax weak.

III.

PSALM LXXVII. 11–20.

11, 12. " *I will remember the works of the Lord : surely I will remember Thy wonders of old. I will meditate also of all Thy work, and talk of Thy doings.*"

Reviving faith returns to God, and drooping doubts are cast aside. It flies on renovated wings to contemplate God's wonder-working hand. It enters the precious treasury full of past records. Here it finds renewal of assurance. Happy meditation traverses the path impressed by heavenly footsteps. Thus refreshed, it opens the mouth in edifying converse. They that fear the Lord will speak often one to another. The words of their mouths, as well as the meditation of their hearts, will be acceptable in His sight. To God also thanksgivings ascend. The knowledge of His glorious works is fruitful parent of adoration.

13. " *Thy way, O God, is in the sanctuary ; who is so great a God as our God ?* "

The footsteps of the Lord are clearly seen in the ordinances of His house. It is the school of heavenly lessons. There His Word reveals His character. There intelligence illumines devout worshippers. They contemplate with open eyes God's majesty, and glory, and grace, and love. The thought cannot be repressed that His every attribute is infinite. Where is greatness like unto His greatness! What power can be compared to His ! To know Him is to lie low at His feet in boundless adoration.

14, 15. "*Thou art the God that doest wonders; Thou hast declared Thy strength among the people. Thou hast with Thine arm redeemed Thy people, the sons of Jacob and Joseph.*"

His sublime works shine as the mid-day sun. His omnipotence appears as an impregnable shield and an all-conquering sword. His' omnipotence is as strong now as in the days of old. His arm has been displayed in redeeming His chosen people from the furnace of affliction, and from the iron grasp of relentless foes. But this power most brightly shines in redeeming His own from the powers of darkness, and saving them from the chains of the arch-enemy of souls. In contemplation of this work the shout breaks forth, "Who is so great a God as our God!"

16, 17, 18. "*The waters saw thee, O God, the waters saw thee; they were afraid: the depths also were troubled. The clouds poured out water; the skies sent out a sound: Thine arrows also went abroad. The voice of Thy thunder was in the heaven: the lightnings lightened the world: the earth trembled and shook.*"

The waters of the sea opposed a barrier to the flying hosts. Deep billows interdicted an advance. But God appears: they tremble and retreat; they leave a dry passage. Throughout, too, the march in the wilderness, all nature seemed arrayed to discomfit the opponents of God's people. A deluge poured down from above. The skies peeled with appalling sounds. The thunder and lightning fought on their behalf. So, too, by prodigies warring on their side, the people were established in the land of Canaan.

19, 20. "*Thy way is in the sea, and Thy path in the*

great waters, and Thy footsteps are not known.   Thou leddest Thy people like a flock by the hand of Moses and Aaron."

The ways of the Lord are past finding out.   It is our wisdom to trust, when we have no skill to trace. Who could have imagined the dividing of the waters of the sea !   The like had never before been seen !   Faith learns the happy lesson, that though God's dealings are inscrutable, no impossibilities can impede Him.   The good Shepherd will be a faithful guardian of His flock. At His will He can raise up ministers to be their guide. As Moses and Aaron went before the rescued hosts, so appointed leaders shall watch over His people.   Let none distrust who have this God for their God.

IV.

PSALM LXXVIII. 1-25.

WE are enjoined to give earnest heed to the words
spoken from heaven. A dark display of Israel's ingratitude and rebellion follows. God's repeated and
abundant mercies seem only to awaken evil. May the
sad example be a profitable warning!

1, 2, 3, 4, 5, 6. " *Give ear, O my people, to my law :
incline your ears to the words of my mouth.   I will open
my mouth in a parable : I will utter dark sayings of
old : which we have heard and known, and our fathers
have told us.   We will not hide them from their children,
showing to the generation to come the praises of the Lord,
and His strength, and His wonderful works that He
hath done.   For He established a testimony in Jacob, and
appointed a law in Israel, which He commanded our
fathers, that they should make them known to their children : that the generation to come might know them, even
the children which should be born : who should arise and
declare them to their children.*"

This introduction claims especial notice. We often
crave audience of God. He here calls us to incline our
ears to His instruction. Let us be quick to hear. His
revelation is the truth of truths, the light of light, the
joy of joys, wisdom in the highest. Not only should
we read, and mark, and learn ; we should impress these

doctrines on our offspring. Fathers should teach their children; and children's children should in turn transmit.

7, 8, 9, 10, 11. " *That they might set their hope in God, and not forget the works of God, but keep His commandments: and might not be as their fathers, a stubborn and rebellious generation; a generation that set not their heart aright, and whose spirit was not stedfast with God. The children of Ephraim, being armed, and carrying bows, turned back in the day of battle. They kept not the covenant of God, and refused to walk in His law; and forgat His works, and His wonders that He had shewed them.*"

Bible-study quickens grace. By pondering God's works of old, confidence will strengthen and hope become more bright. We shall tremble, too, at the awful iniquity of Israel's sons. They quenched the recollection of the repeated mercies, which blessed their fathers. Armour was provided for them, but they refused to stand firm, and fled before their foes. They closed their eyes, and would not see His arm extended for their help.

12, 13, 14, 15, 16. " *Marvellous things did He in the sight of their fathers, in the land of Egypt, in the field of Zoan. He divided the sea, and caused them to pass through; and He made the waters to stand as an heap. In the day-time also He led them with a cloud, and all the night with a light of fire. He clave the rocks in the wilderness, and gave them drink as out of the great depths. He brought streams also out of the rock, and caused waters to run down like rivers.*"

A recapitulation follows of the wonders which

cradled the childhood of His people. In this history, God's character—His love, His might—is written as with a sunbeam. No enemies could crush. No perils could destroy. Impossibilities vanished. He made the waters of the deep to be a highway for their feet. The mighty billows stood as a wall on their right hand and on their left. That their journey might be safe, a cloud from heaven preceded their march by day, and a canopy of fire shone over them at night. Does thirst oppress them ? The hard rock opens its flinty sides, and refreshing streams flow in their rear. Miracle followed miracle, proclaiming His unceasing care.

17, 18, 19, 20, 21, 22, 23, 24, 25. "*And they sinned yet more against Him by provoking the most High in the wilderness. And they tempted God in their heart by asking meat for their lust. Yea, they spake against God : they said, Can God furnish a table in the wilderness? Behold, He smote the rock, that the waters gushed out, and the streams overflowed ; can He give bread also ? can He provide flesh for His people ? Therefore the Lord heard this, and was wroth : so a fire was kindled against Jacob, and anger also came up against Israel ; because they believed not in God, and trusted not in His salvation, Though He had commanded the clouds from above, and opened the doors of heaven, and had rained down manna upon them to eat, and had given them of the corn of heaven. Man did eat angels' food : He sent them meat to the full.*"

Can it be that such miracles of love could fail to melt their hearts ; and that such evidence of fatherly guardianship should suffer rebellion still to live ! Alas !

abundant kindness awakened superabundant sin! They
sneered at past loving-kindness. They allowed that
their thirst had been relieved ; but they doubted
whether meat could similarly be provided! Can we
marvel that God's wrath went forth, and that fire
raged in their camp? While we bless God for His
goodness, let us remember that to hardened rebels He
is a consuming fire.

V.

PSALM LXXVIII. 26–48.

26, 27, 28, 29. "*He caused an east wind to blow in the heaven: and by His power He brought in the south wind. He rained flesh also upon them as dust, and feathered fowls like as the sand of the sea. And He let it fall in the midst of their camp, round about their habitations. So they did eat, and were well filled; for He gave them their own desire; they were not estranged from their lust.*"

How striking is this instance of God's forbearance! Tender compassion checks the outbursts of just vengeance. Instead of punishing, He gratifies their impious desires. He sent the food which they believed He could not grant. He multiplied it beyond their power to gather. They fed until their appetite was more than sated.

30, 31, 32. "*But while their meat was yet in their mouths, the wrath of God came upon them, and slew the fattest of them, and smote down the chosen men of Israel. For all this they sinned still, and believed not for His wondrous works.*"

Let presumptuous rebels tremble. Wrath may linger, but delay is not forgiveness. In due time it will blaze forth, and terrible will be the results. The awful sequel shows this truth. While they feasted, vengeance fell. The richest and the mightiest found no refuge in their high estate. They perished with the lowest in the camp. But the hard hearts, unmelted by the plenty, and unappalled by wrath, waxed more daring in rebellious feeling. They had no confidence in His goodness, no fear of His anger. Reprobate is the case which neither mercy nor displeasure leads to submission.

33, 34, 35, 36, 37. " *Therefore their days did He consume in vanity, and their years in trouble. When He slew them, then they sought Him ; and they returned and enquired early after God. And they remembered that God was their rock, and the high God their redeemer. Nevertheless they did flatter Him with their mouth, and they lied unto Him with their tongues. For their heart was not right with Him, neither were they stedfast in His covenant.*"

Their troubles were continued. The scourge drove them to seek relief; but their outward change was not inward conversion. In semblance they became other men; but the same features were behind the mask. With utterance they seemingly drew near; but falsehood dwelt on their lips. They were not slow to promise; but their unstable minds were like the leaking sieve. They made a covenant; but it was only to break it.

38, 39, 40, 41. " *But He, being full of compassion, forgave their iniquity, and destroyed them not ; yea, many a time turned He His anger away, and did not stir up all His wrath. For He remembered that they were but flesh; a wind that passeth away, and cometh not again. How oft did they provoke Him in the wilderness, and grieve Him in the desert ! Yea, they turned back and tempted God, and limited the Holy One of Israel.*"

But still compassion is not utterly exhausted. Our God is infinite in all His attributes. He pitied them still, and held back the arm uplifted to destroy. He remembered their utter feebleness. For a little season only they sojourned on earth. We hear the wind, but it soon is gone. So from this scene they would be quickly taken, and their places would be no more found. To enumerate their sins exceeds all power. So, too, to enumerate God's acts of goodness. While we shudder at their vileness, let us adore forbearing mercy.

42, 43, 44, 45, 46, 47, 48. " *They remembered not His hand, nor the day when He delivered them from the enemy. How He had wrought His signs in Egypt, and His wonders in the field of Zoan: And had turned their rivers into blood; and their floods that they could not drink. He sent divers sorts of flies among them; which devoured them; and frogs, which destroyed them. He gave also their increase unto the caterpillar, and their labour unto the locust. He destroyed their vines with hail, and their sycamore trees with frost. He gave up their cattle also to the hail, and their flocks to hot thunderbolts.*"

Great had been their deliverance. They well knew God's terrible acts upon their foes. He had shown that all instruments of vengeance subserved His will. All creation at His bidding would arise to plague. Their annals were the record of His power to avenge. But vain was the lesson. Provocation was their rule.

VI.

PSALM LXXVIII. 49–72.

49, 50, 51. "*He cast upon them the fierceness of His anger, wrath, and indignation, and trouble, by sending evil angels among them. He made a way to His anger; He spared not their soul from death, but gave their life over to the pestilence; and smote all the first-born in Egypt; the chief of their strength in the tabernacles of Ham.*"

Wrath terribly smote Egypt. Every form of plague spread desolation. All agents of evil did their ruthless work. Misery reached its height when the first-born fell, and death was the inmate of each home. The evidence is clear that God, who delights in mercy, can righteously execute severity. Ah, sin! what hast thou done? Let us ponder and be wise!

52, 53, 54, 55. "*But made His own people to go forth like sheep, and guided them in the wilderness like a flock. And He led them on safely, so that they feared not: but the sea overwhelmed their enemies. And He brought them to the border of His sanctuary, even to this mountain, which His right hand had purchased. He cast out the heathen also before them, and divided them an inheritance by line, and made the tribes of Israel to dwell in their tents.*"

It is sweet to return to views of God's gracious dealings. Behold Him guiding His own from this land of thraldom, as a shepherd tending his beloved flock. Behold Him preceding through the wilderness, and bring-

ing them safely to the promised land. Behold Him
driving the natives from their land, that Israel's tribes
might settle in the goodly heritage. The history is an
assurance that He will safely bring His own to the
heavenly rest.

56, 57, 58. " *Yet they tempted and provoked the most
high God, and kept not His testimonies. But turned back,
and dealt unfaithfully like their fathers : they were turned
aside like a deceitful bow. For they provoked Him to
anger with their high places, and moved Him to jealousy
with their graven images.*"

Can it be that a people thus favoured can forget their
God, reject His testimonies, and provoke Him by
idolatries ! Alas ! what evil will not man perpetrate !
God was deserted. Altars to idols were erected.

59, 60, 61, 62, 63, 64. "*When God heard this He
was wroth, and greatly abhorred Israel. So that He
forsook the tabernacle of Shiloh, the tent which He placed
among men ; and delivered His strength into captivity,
and His glory into the enemy's hand. He gave His
people over also unto the sword ; and was wroth with
His inheritance. The fire consumed their young men ;
and their maidens were not given to marriage. Their
priests fell by the sword ; and their widows made no
lamentation.*"

Warnings are here multiplied. God saw Israel's rebellion and raised the arm of vengeance. The tabernacle of His presence was deserted. The enemy came
in like a flood. The inheritance was laid waste.
Misery consumed the flower of their youth. Oh ! let
us dread the wrath of God. We are warned that He
marks and punishes iniquity.

65, 66. " *Then the Lord awaked as one out of sleep,
and like a mighty man that shouteth by reason of wine.
And He smote His enemies in the hinder parts ; He put
them to a perpetual reproach."*

Here evidence returns that free grace reigns. Mercy
rejects slumber. God is aroused and drives back the
insulting foe. He inflicts terrible chastisement. When
His people merit extremities of wrath, love will still
love them.

67, 68, 69. "*Moreover, He refused the tabernacle of
Joseph, and chose not the tribe of Ephraim. But chose
the tribe of Judah, the Mount Zion which He loved.
And He built His sanctuary like high palaces, like the
earth which He hath established for ever."*

The tribe at first so honoured receives mark of
rejection. The Temple must not rise in Shiloh.
Joseph must be humbled, and Judah must be honoured
with distinguishing favour. The Ark must be removed
to rest on Mount Zion, and there the Temple—the joy
of the whole earth—must show its glorious front. Let
us again take warning. The Gospel is not restricted to
one place. If it be not gladly welcomed and devoutly
honoured, God may remove it, and gladden others with
the sound.

70, 71, 72. " *He chose David also His servant, and
took him from the sheepfolds : from following the ewes
great with young He brought him to feed Jacob His
people, and Israel His inheritance. So he fed them
according to the integrity of his heart ; and guided
them by the skilfulness of his hands."*

God's mercy leaves not His people without the
guidance of a wise Prince. He chooses David. He

raises him from low estate, and places him on a high
throne.   He gives him skill and wisdom to rule
in righteousness.   Here we have our rightful King.
The government is on the shoulders of our Jesus.   Let
us fall low before Him : and serve Him faithfully and
love Him supremely.   To us He is the King of kings,
and Lord of lords.

VII.

PSALM LXXIX.

THE ruins of the Temple and the cruelties of the insulting foe impel to the mercy-seat. Promises of praise are uttered. In the depths of distress may we thus seek and vow!

1. " *O God, the heathen are come into Thine inheritance ; Thy holy temple have they defiled ; they have laid Jerusalem on heaps.*"

With tearful eye the pious Israelite beholds the desolation of his hallowed places. He would move mournfully amid the ruins of his beloved city. Can it be that the Temple has thus fallen! Can it be that the protecting walls are thus laid low! Have the heathen thus triumphed! Is the chosen city thus deserted! Such thoughts of anguish naturally arise amid the desolate scene.

2, 3. " *The dead bodies of Thy servants have they given to be meat unto the fowls of the heaven, the flesh of Thy saints unto the beasts of the earth. Their blood have they shed like water round about Jerusalem ; and there was none to bury them.*"

Cruel carnage marked the invader's course. The slaughtered were exposed to vilest indignities. Devouring birds mangled the neglected corpses; ravenous beasts rioted in the abundance of their prey. Blood flowed in copious streams, and no survivors could inter the dead.

4. " *We are become a reproach to our neighbours, a scorn and derision to them that are round about us.*"

The neighbouring nations, which once viewed Jerusalem as the perfection of strength and beauty, and feared her as the mistress of the earth, now sneered at her fallen state. No tender pity softened their hearts. Derision sat upon their lips.

5. "*How long, Lord? wilt Thou be angry for ever? shall Thy jealousy burn like fire?*"

The period of calamity seemed endless. It is traced to its real cause. God's displeasure has poured down these miseries. The cry goes up to Him for intermission. It cries, Let not Thine anger be thus prolonged; let it not burn like an unextinguishable flame. It is our wisdom when lying in the depths of sorrow thus to plead.

6, 7. " *Pour out Thy wrath upon the heathen that have not known Thee, and upon the kingdoms that have not called upon Thy name: for they have devoured Jacob, and laid waste his dwelling-place.*"

Prayer beseeches God to mark that the triumphant nations were also enemies to Him. They knew not His majesty and glory. They had never acknowledged Him as their God. It is the province of faith to appeal to God that we are truly His, and that they who hate us honour not His glorious name.

8, 9. " *O remember not against us former iniquities: let Thy tender mercies speedily prevent us; for we are brought very low. Help us, O God of our salvation, for the glory of Thy name; and deliver us, and purge away our sins, for Thy name's sake.*"

The remembrance of former iniquities should ever be

before our eyes. Our cry should be that mercy would heal these wounds. Our only plea should be that God would thus glorify His great name, and make us monuments of His redeeming powers.

10, 11, 12. *" Wherefore should the heathen say, Where is their God? let Him be known among the heathen in our sight by the revenging of the blood of Thy servants which is shed. Let the sighing of the prisoner come before Thee; according to the greatness of Thy power preserve Thou those that are appointed to die; and render unto our neighbours seven-fold into their bosom their reproach, wherewith they have reproached Thee, O Lord."*

Let not the sneer prevail that God has cast off His own. Rather let His glory be conspicuous in the ruin of the blood-stained foes. Let the plaintive wails of the captives prevail, and let the death-doomed find deliverance.

13. *" So we Thy people, and sheep of Thy pasture, will give Thee thanks for ever: we will show forth Thy praise to all generations."*

The happy result shall be constant flow of grateful praises from generation to generation. A ransomed flock shall magnify the Lord.

VIII.

PSALM LXXX.

SUPPLIANTS in deep misery flee to the mercy-seat. A graphic allegory portrays the Church. May we bear fruit as lively branches of the true Vine!

1, 2. *" Give ear, O Shepherd of Israel, Thou that leadest Joseph like a flock; Thou that dwellest between the cherubim, shine forth. Before Ephraim and Benjamin and Manasseh, stir up Thy strength, and come and save us."*

In terms tender and urgent the heavenly Shepherd is implored to watch over His beloved flock. He is invoked, too, as the God whose presence sanctified the mercy-seat. When the tabernacle moved the tribes of Ephraim, Benjamin and Manasseh brought up the rear, and so were the nearest to the cherubim overshadowing the Ark. Thus the symbol of His presence was contiguous to these tribes. Let us profit by this invocation. In our distresses—and they may be very many—let us think of the Good Shepherd, and remind Him of His tender love. Let us think of our God upon His mercy-seat, and beseech Him to manifest His strength.

3. *" Turn us again, O God, and cause Thy face to shine; and we shall be saved."*

The confession is implied that we drink the cup of sorrow because of our wanderings from God. The supplication sounds, that He would, in His full mercy,

bring us back, and·chase away our gloom by the shin-
ings of His smile. If He vouchsafes to grant this
mercy, perils and destruction flee away, and we stand
immovably on salvation's ground.

4, 5, 6, 7. *" O Lord God of Hosts, how long wilt Thou
be angry against the prayer of Thy people ? Thou feedest
them with the bread of tears; and givest them tears to
drink in great measure. Thou makest us a strife unto
our neighbours; and our enemies laugh among themselves.
Turn us again, O God of hosts, and cause Thy face to
shine; and we shall be saved."*

Penitential prayer had sued, but answers lingered.
Fast-flowing tears bedewed the cheeks. Needful food
was mingled with bitter tokens of affliction. In importunity God is besought no longer to delay His aid.
Not only did a wounded conscience utter words of
sorrow. The surrounding nations also marked their
calamities, and heaped derision on the downcast people.
The cry is renewed, Turn us again, O God of hosts,
and cause Thy face to shine; and we shall be saved.
If delay occurs, let it quicken our earnestness.

8, 9, 10, 11. *" Thou hast brought a vine out of Egypt :
Thou hast cast out the heathen, and planted it. Thou
preparedst room before it, and didst cause it to take deep
root, and it filled the land. The hills were covered with
the shadow of it, and the boughs thereof were like the
goodly cedars. ·She sent out her boughs unto the sea, and
her branches unto the river."*

In the midst of suffering it is salutary to revisit
times of joy and gladness. Israel recalls God's early
favour. He brought His people like a tender plant
from Egypt's soil. He removed the heathen, and planted

it in earth's loveliest spot. Here it took root and sent forth luxuriant branches. Such mercies now were recalled by their mourning hearts. The contrast awakened a plaintive cry.

12, 13, 14, 15, 16. " *Why hast thou then broken down her hedges, so that all they which pass by the way do pluck her ? The boar out of the wood doth waste it, and the wild beast of the field doth devour it. Return, we beseech Thee, O God of hosts: look down from heaven, and behold, and visit this vine ; and the vineyard which Thy right hand hath planted, and the branch that Thou madest strong for Thyself. It is burnt with fire ; it is cut down : they perish at the rebuke of Thy countenance.*"

The present desolation shows a terrible reverse. Protecting barriers are levelled. All passengers may pillage as they please. Wild ·animals may devour the fruits. Again prayer beseeches God to return and visit His ravaged vine. In remembrance of former mercies, let us pray that He who hath begun a good work in us will perform it until the day of Christ.

17, 18, 19. " *Let Thy hand be upon the Man of Thy right hand, upon the Son of Man whom Thou madest strong for Thyself. So will not we go back from Thee : quicken us, and we will call upon Thy name. Turn us again, O Lord God of hosts, cause Thy face to shine ; and we shall be saved.*"

Hope now brightens. The eye rests on Jesus. God is besought to uphold His beloved Son endued with all strength to save us. He will restore our souls. Quickened by His grace, prayers shall continue to wrestle with Him for renewed succour. Repetition proves the earnestness of the soul.

IX.

PSALM LXXXI.

OBSERVANCE of public ordinances is enjoined. The path of obedience is the path of blessedness. May we hearken unto our God; He will appear rich to multiply mercies.

1, 2, 3. *"Sing aloud unto God our strength: make a joyful noise unto the God of Jacob. Take a psalm and bring hither the timbrel, the pleasant harp with the psaltery. Blow up the trumpet in the new moon, in the time appointed, on our solemn feast day."*

It is a constant duty publicly to worship God, and to assemble in joyful crowds within the sanctuary. It runs on through the year's course. But there are especial times which should awaken especial thanksgivings. It is most wise to celebrate appointed seasons with all the aids which reverence can bring. Thus gratitude and love will kindle into brighter flame, and sense of mercies will take deeper root. Thus shall we meeten for the day when every crown shall be cast at the Redeemer's feet, and endless Hallelujahs issue from all lips.

4, 5. *"For this was a statute for Israel, and a law of the God of Jacob. This he ordained in Joseph for a testimony, when he went out through the land of Egypt; where I heard a language that I understood not."*

Such service was enjoined to the elders of faith's house. It was ordained to promote their wisdom, joy, and profit. Doubtless the true light now brightly shines, and we have passed from the shadowy forms of types and emblematic worship. But the essence of true religion abides the same. If forms are not observed, reality may soon be lost. We are called to note the period when these injunctions were given. It was at the moment of their deliverance from the slavery of Egypt: from the oppression of those who were aliens both in heart and tongue.

6, 7. "*I removed his shoulder from the burden: his hands were delivered from the pots. Thou calledst in trouble, and I delivered thee; I answered thee in the secret place of thunder; I proved thee at the waters of Meribah.*"

Grievous burdens oppressed the groaning people, but God delivered them, and their servile bondage ended. In the wilderness trouble continued; but from the cloud—the home of thunders—answers responded to their cry, and faith grew strong by frequent trial.

8, 9, 10. "*Hear, O my people, and I will testify unto thee: O Israel, if thou wilt hearken unto me; there shall no strange god be in thee; neither shalt thou worship any strange god. I am the Lord thy God, which brought thee out of the land of Egypt : open thy mouth wide, and I will fill it.*"

The Lord tenderly expostulates. He stoops to crave attention. He assures them that if they would obey, He, and He alone, would be their God, and no vile deluders should mislead them. He reminds them that He is the same God who wrought such wonders for them in their early days. He assures them that He is the same in the infinitudes of His love and power; that they were not straitened in Him; that if they would be willing to receive, He would fill them until no more could be contained. Let us thus open our hearts, and doubt not that He will fully occupy.

11, 12. "*But my people would not hearken to my voice; and Israel would none of me. So I gave them up unto their own hearts' lust : and they walked in their own counsels.*"

We shudder at the madness of rebellious man. He closes his ears : he rejects God, and thus God leaves him. Terrible curses follow. The decree goes forth, Ephraim is joined to idols : let him alone.

13, 14, 15, 16. "*Oh that my people had hearkened unto me, and Israel had walked in my ways ! I should soon have subdued their enemies, and turned my hand against their adversaries. The haters of the Lord should have submitted themselves unto Him : but their time should have endured for ever. He should have fed them also with the finest of the wheat : and with honey out of the rock should I have satisfied thee.*"

Mournful is this upbraiding note. The scene is darkened by a picture of the blessedness thus forfeited. No mercy would have been withheld from the obedient. Their enemies would have fallen low before them. There would have been no evening to their bright days of joy. Their life would have been a perpetual feast. Their table would have been luxuriantly spread by God's own hand. Let us be wise, and hearken diligently, that we may enjoy such blessedness.

X.

PSALM LXXXII.

God's supremacy over all magistrates is declared.   Un-
just judges are reproved, and prayer is made that God
would maintain justice.

---

1. "*God standeth in the congregation of the mighty ;
He judgeth among the gods.*"

Man raised to a seat of pre-eminence is prone to
forget the hand which thus uplifts.   His boastful heart
regards the power as his own prerogative, and rules
as if accountable to none.   But God's kingdom reigns
over all.   Earthly authority emanates from Him.   In
courts of judicature He is supreme.   His eye discerns
the movement of each heart.   His hand is ready to
control.   The wicked Sanhedrim little thought of the
presence of the Lord of all.   The unrighteous Pilate
felt not that he could have no power at all except what
was given him from above.

2. "*How long will ye judge unjustly, and accept the
persons of the wicked ?*"

God condescends to expostulate.   He upbraids the
folly of injustice.   It is sin in His sight to regard the
persons of men rather than the cause of truth.   Let us
remember that a day is coming when a righteous
tribunal shall be erected ; when a righteous Judge
shall sit, whose sceptre is a right sceptre—whose right

hand is full of righteousness. On that day a crown of
righteousness will be accorded to His faithful followers.

3, 4. " *Defend the poor and fatherless ; do justice to the
afflicted and needy.   Deliver the poor and needy : rid
them out of the hand of the wicked.*"

The principles are declared which should regulate
the halls of justice. On the bench the poor should ever
see the guardian of their rights. They who have no
interest from wealth and station should feel that they
are safe in rulers who regard not station and despise
the bribe. Happy are the courts in which pure justice
reigns, and happy the people who are thus ruled!
The thought cannot be checked; happy are they who
from their hearts can say to Jesus, We believe that
Thou shalt come to be our Judge. We well know that
Thou wilt deliver us from oppression, and keep that
which we have committed unto Thee.

5. " *They know not, neither will they understand ;
they walk on in darkness : all the foundations of the
earth are out of course.*"

Injustice springs from an unenlightened heart. If
eyes were opened from above, it would be quickly seen
that it is wisdom to love truth. But darkness too often
spreads its blinding power. Confusion is the sure
result ! The very earth seems tottering. It rests on
no stability. Again we feel that they dwell safely on
a rock for whom God's right hand orders events righteously.

6, 7. " *I have said, Ye are gods : and all of you are
children of the Most High.   But ye shall die like men,
and fall like one of the princes.*"

God again reminds that all authority is from Him.

He calls magistrates to rule in His name. He confers titles which show that they must be honoured as His deputed officers. But though thus raised, their original is dust and ashes. They soon will crumble in their native earth. The great ones who preceded them had been stripped of all external show, and laid in the humble grave. They, too, must fall. Where then will be their supremacy? Wise only are the earthly judges who hear God's judgment-trumpet sounding in their ears.

8. " *Arise, O God, judge the earth: for Thou shalt inherit all nations.*"

From this contemplation faith gladly turns ro God. The cry goes forth that He would quickly take to Himself His great power and reign: and mould all hearts to be submissive to His will. May glorious prospects gladden our transported gaze, when we pray, Thy kingdom come.

XI.

PSALM LXXXIII.

GOD is called to mark the confederacy of the ungodly, and to avenge His cause as in times of old. God thus appearing shall be acknowledged as Jehovah.

1. "*Keep not Thou silence, O God ; hold not Thy peace, and be not still, O God.*"

It is the happy privilege of faith to deal familiarly at the mercy-seat. As a child it may boldly cling to a loving Father. With importunity it may crave attention. It may give God no rest until His power is displayed. Thus God is here implored to raise His voice against the enemies of His kingdom.

2. "*For, lo, Thine enemies make a tumult ; and they that hate Thee have lifted up the head.*"

Shall God be silent, while they that hate Him are loud in insults ? Shall He sit indifferent, while the earth rings with the tumult of rebellion ? Speak, Lord, Thy voice causes earth to be mute.

3, 4, 5. "*They have taken crafty counsel against Thy people, and consulted against Thy hidden ones. They have said, Come, and let us cut them off from being a nation ; that the name of Israel may be no more in remembrance. For they have consulted together with one consent : they are confederate against Thee.*"

Not only do they loudly rave ; they plot in secresy,

VOL. II.   C and craftily devise rebellious plans. Hate is the moving principle within. It is misery to them that God's people live, are honoured and exhibit power. In dark conclave they consult to extinguish their name, and to bury them in oblivion. But God watches His hidden ones. They may not be conspicuous upon earth. No pomp may signalize their course. No grandeur may court homage. But God has known them before the world's birth, and will in due time proclaim them as kings and princes to Himself. Let none of His children complain that their way is hidden from their God. He has graven them on the palms .of His hands. They shall shine brightly in the day when He makes up His jewels. .

6, 7, 8. " *The tabernacles of Edom, and the Ishmaelites, of Moab and the Hagarenes ; Gebal, and Ammon, and Amalek ; the Philistines, with the inhabitants of Tyre ; Assur also is joined with them : they have holpen the children of Lot.*"

If God knows His meek and humble followers, and calls them all by their names, so, too, He well knows the multitude of confederate hosts. The catalogue of Israel's adversaries classified by name, proves that the haters of God are individually perceived. The powers allied against Israel were all overthrown. Separately they perished. So all God's enemies shall be arraigned in distinct personality, and each shall receive his due reward. They will each hear, O thou wicked one, thus and thus hast thou done ; thus and thus must thou be requited. Crowds shall not hide individuality.

9, 10, 11, 12. " *Do unto them as unto the Midianites; as to Sisera, as to Jabin, at the brook of Kison : which*

perished at Endor; they became as dung for the earth.
Make their nobles like Oreb and like Zeeb; yea, all their
princes as Zebah and as Zalmunna; who said, Let us
take to ourselves the houses of God in possession."

It is true piety to remind God of His former deeds of
wrath, and to implore Him again to do as He has done.

13, 14, 15, 16, 17. *"O my God, make them like a*
wheel; as the stubble before the wind. As the fire
burneth a wood, and as the flame setteth the mountains
on fire; so persecute them with Thy tempest, and make
them afraid with Thy storm. Fill their faces with shame,
that they may seek Thy name, O Lord. Let them be con-
founded and troubled for ever; yea, let them be put to
shame, and perish."

Graphic images show the weakness of rebellious men.
Their stability is as a rolling wheel. Their firmness
drifts as stubble before the wind. They yield as the
trees of the forest to the power of devouring flame.
God is besought to overthrow them with shame, that
they may humbly seek His knowledge.

18. *"That men may know that Thou, whose name*
alone is Jehovah, art the Most High over all the earth."

The ultimate desire is that He who alone bears the
incommunicable name of Jehovah, the self-existent,
and the cause of all life, may be exalted above all the
earth, and that every tongue may praise, and honour,
and adore Him. In accordance may the longings of
our hearts be to magnify His name.

XII.

PSALM LXXXIV.

LONGING desires are expressed for the joy of public ordinances. The happiness is extolled of those who frequent God's court. The God, who hears and answers prayer, is magnified.

-----

1. " *How amiable are Thy tabernacles, O Lord of hosts!*"
The Psalmist speaks as one far distant from the hill of Zion. He remembers the delight of gazing on the beauteous Temple. The very sight had kindled love and devotion. In the fervour of retrospective ecstasy he extols the much-loved spectacle. May the sight of every consecrated fane fill us with adoring thoughts of Him whose worship there is sought!

2. " *My soul longeth, yea, even fainteth for the courts of the Lord ; my heart and my flesh crieth out for the living God.*"
Passionate expressions pour forth intense desire for the enjoyment of God's presence in the sanctuary. The heart burns with longings; the internal feeling is warmly exhibited. May the like feeling ever swell within us!

3. " *Yea, the sparrow hath found an house, and the swallow a nest for herself, where she may lay her young, even Thine altars, O Lord of hosts, my King, and my God.*"
Some obscurity may hide the precise significance of

this poetic image. Let us be content to gain edification. Regard the birds of the air. They seek and find some secret places of repose, where they may rest in calm security and nestle with their infant brood. Thus our souls should find their tranquil home in nearness to their King and their God.

4, 5, 6, 7. " *Blessed are they that dwell in Thy house ; they will be still praising Thee. Blessed is the man whose strength is in Thee; in whose heart are the ways of them. Who passing through the valley of Baca make it a well: the rain also filleth the pools. They go from strength to strength ; every one of them in Zion appeareth before God.*"

We see the picture of the tribes pursuing their journey to the great festivals at Jerusalem. They faint not, neither are weary. The needful strength is supplied. They are upheld in the journey. A gloomy valley must be passed, but in it they find refreshment. Water fails not. The wells have been replenished by the seasonable rains. Their limbs each day are girded with fresh strength. At last each pious Israelite safely treads the sanctuary for which his heart had panted. This is a picture of believers toiling through the march of life. The way is sometimes long ; dark valleys must be passed, but sweet streams are ever near. Needful vigour is maintained. The heavenly Zion is surely reached. No pilgrim has perished on the road. They went forth to go into the land of Canaan, and into the land of Canaan they came.

8. " *O Lord God of hosts, hear my prayer: give ear, O God of Jacob.*"

In such prospect who will not cry, Give ear, O God

of Jacob, listen to my cry, and bring me safely to Thy longed-for home?

9, 10. *" Behold, O God our shield, and look upon the face of Thine anointed. For a day in Thy courts is better than a thousand: I had rather be a doorkeeper in the house of my God, than to dwell in the tents of wickedness."*

It is good to cause our pilgrimage to resound with prayer, and ever to recognize God's protecting presence. It is good to remind Him that we have the unction of the Holy One, and have received the earnest of heaven into our hearts. It is good to add that we prefer the lowest station in His courts to the highest splendours of stately palaces. Let us be followers of Moses, who chose rather to suffer affliction with the people of God than to enjoy the pleasures of sin for a season, esteeming the reproach of Christ greater riches than the treasures of Egypt; for he had respect unto the recompense of the reward.

11, 12. *" For the Lord God is a sun and shield: the Lord will give grace and glory: no good thing will He withhold from them that walk uprightly. O Lord of hosts, blessed is the man that trusteth in Thee."*

Who is a God like unto our God? What can we require that is not ours in Him? What is the sun to the world? What is the shield in the day of battle? All this and more than this He is to us. What can they need, from whom no good thing is withheld? May the Spirit guide us to walk uprightly! Then shall we inherit the blessedness of all who trust in Him.

XIII.

PSALM LXXXV.

BRIGHT views of redeeming love shine forth in the opening of this Psalm. Prayer is made that grace may still abound. God's attributes are shown to be all reconciled in Christ. May we gaze with delight, and give all glory to our God!

1, 2, 3. "*Lord, Thou hast been favourable unto Thy land: Thou hast brought back the captivity of Jacob. Thou hast forgiven the iniquity of Thy people: Thou hast covered all their sin. Thou hast taken away all Thy wrath: Thou hast turned Thyself from the fierceness of Thine anger.*"

The immediate occasion of this triumphant joy is doubtless the deliverance of Israel's sons from some oppressing enemy. But the predictive shadow is soon chased away by the bright shining of redemption's rescue. In this scheme the riches of God's grace are seen. Free favour comes forth mighty to save. The wonders of mercy are ascribed to this love as their source. We see the origin of complete salvation. Wrath had existed against all sin; anger had fiercely blazed against iniquity; but vengeance is quenched in the ocean of redeeming blood. Where is iniquity? It is all forgiven. Where are sins? They are all covered. Let our rejoicing souls testify, Lord, Thou hast been favourable unto us.

4, 5, 6, 7. "*Turn us, O God of our salvation, and
cause Thine anger toward us to cease. Wilt Thou be
angry with us for ever? wilt Thou draw out Thine anger
to all generations? Wilt Thou not revive us again, that
Thy people may rejoice in Thee? Show us Thy mercy,
O Lord, and grant us Thy salvation.*"

But the ransomed heritage often fails to realize secured
salvation. They tremble lest God's anger should return, and favour cease to smile. Let this temptation
always drive to prayer. This is the time to supplicate
that dying graces may revive, and that joy and gladness
may reoccupy the soul; that mercy may again abound;
and that salvation's glories may illustriously shine.

8. "*I will hear what God the Lord will speak: for
He will speak peace unto His people, and to His saints:
but let them not turn again to folly.*"

Answers will surely come. Let us open wide our
hearts to welcome their arrival. They will fly on the
wings of peace. The voice will be heard, Peace I
leave with you; My peace I give unto you. The Lord
of peace Himself will give us peace always by all means.
But let us take heed, and never turn aside to folly's
fears and doubts and ways. Let us ever listen to
wisdom's teaching, and walk in wisdom's ways.

9, 10. "*Surely His salvation is nigh them that fear
Him; that glory may dwell in our land. Mercy and
truth are met together; righteousness and peace have
kissed each other.*"

It is rich mercy that salvation is not to be sought
in a far-distant region. Tedious efforts and protracted
wanderings are not needed. It is ever by our side.

We may open the hand and take it. What a constellation of blessedness brightens in the thought! Mercy, which ever pitifully yearns, has ample scope. Truth hastens to meet her with the assurance that it no more opposes. Righteousness enrobes the ransomed flock. All heaven is at peace, and all God's attributes embrace. Oh! blessed Jesus, we adore Thee for thy saving work!

11, 12, 13. *" Truth shall spring out of the earth; and righteousness shall look down from heaven. Yea, the Lord shall give that which is good; and our land shall yield her increase. Righteousness shall go before Him, and shall set us in the way of His steps."*

Glorious results follow. On earth truth shall be as a fruitful crop, and righteousness shall flow down as showers from heaven. Every grace shall flourish and abound. The Good Shepherd shall precede His flock, and shall guide them safely in all righteous ways. How glorious is our Gospel, in its origin, in its work, in its effects! May we fully receive it! It is the blessing of blessings.

XIV.

PSALM LXXXVI.

A stream of continuous prayer flows throughout this Psalm. Praise is sweetly intermixed. Pleas for audience are urgently enforced. May we thus pray, and verily we shall be heard!

———

1. " *Bow down Thine ear, O Lord, hear me; for I am poor and needy.*"

The cry is the breathing of humility. To seek help from our own poverty is to draw water from an empty cistern. Let us fly to God's fulness; it ever overflows.

2. " *Preserve my soul, for I am holy: O Thou my God, save Thy servant that trusteth in Thee.*"

Enemies are always near: God only can keep and save. Let us urge the plea, We are Thine by entire surrender of ourselves. All our confidence rests on Thee.

3, 4. " *Be merciful unto me, O Lord : for I cry unto Thee daily. Rejoice the soul of Thy servant : for unto Thee, O Lord, do I lift up my soul.*"

Mercy is our hourly need: for mercy let our hourly cry ascend. We shall hear joy and gladness, if on Him only our eyes are fixed.

5. " *For Thou, Lord, art good, and ready to forgive ; and plenteous in mercy unto all them that call upon Thee.*"

When we thus call upon our God, we only ask for the display of His own heart. Goodness and mercy, grace and love there dwell. O God, give them scope. Let them come forth to help.

6, 7. "*Give ear, O Lord, unto my prayer; and attend to the voice of my supplications. In the day of my trouble I will call upon Thee: for Thou wilt answer me.*"

The cry continues, I cannot let Thee rest. I must take heaven by storm. Awake, awake in my behalf. Troubles abound. But they bear me on their tide to Thee. I come in full assurance that Thy promises shall never fail, and faithful prayer shall never be cast out.

8, 9, 10. "*Among the gods there is none like unto Thee, O Lord; neither are there any works like unto Thy works. All nations whom Thou hast made shall come and worship before Thee, O Lord; and shall glorify Thy name. For Thou art great and doest wondrous things: Thou art God alone.*"

Precious is the season when the eye of faith contemplates the greatness—the majesty—the glory of our God. In heaven and throughout earth He sits supreme, worthy of all praise—all homage—all adoring love! In every clime enlightened servants now bow down to worship Him. The day will come when His knowledge shall cover the earth, even as the waters cover the sea. Then every knee shall bow before Him and every tongue shall magnify His name. O Lord, hasten the blessed time!

11. "*Teach me Thy way, O Lord; I will walk in Thy truth: unite my heart to fear Thy name.*"

How quickly the believer flies back to prayer.   Here
is his solace and his heart's home.   His grand desire
is, that the Lord would instruct him in the path of life.
He has no greater desire than to walk in God's truth.
He feels that his heart is prone in all its parts to
wander.   In itself it has neither cohesion nor stability.
He prays that God would so restrain it by His bands,
that no part should ever deviate from His fear.

12, 13. *" I will praise Thee, O Lord my God, with all
my heart ; and I will glorify Thy name for evermore.
For great is Thy mercy toward me; and Thou hast
delivered my soul from the lowest hell."*

He vows that eternal praise shall issue from his comforted heart.   Such glory is indeed God's due.   For
through redeeming blood He has rescued from perdition's lowest depths.

14, 15. · *O God, the proud are risen against me, and
the assemblies of violent men have sought after my soul,
and have not set Thee before them.   But Thou, O Lord,
art a God full of compassion, and gracious, long-suffering,
and plenteous in mercy and truth."*

In contrast to this mercy the Psalmist sees the
enmity of man.   But he takes refuge in his God.
His compassions never fail; His grace abides for
ever; His long-suffering is inexhaustible ; His mercy
and truth are overflowing.

16, 17. *" O turn unto me, and have mercy upon me ;
give Thy strength unto Thy servant, and save the son of
Thine handmaid.   Show me a token for good; that
they which hate me may see it, and be ashamed ; because
Thou, Lord, hast holpen me, and comforted me."*

This view of God prompts the prayer, that He

would arise and strengthen and save: and give such
tokens of His loving-kindness, that all observers may
perceive that believers are the blessed men receiving
help from heaven, and rejoicing in the Spirit's comforts. When such manifestations abound they cannot
be hidden. Shame depresses the cruel adversaries.
They are constrained to confess, that vain is their
enmity when God extends His hand to work deliverance. May we be monuments of such help!

XV.

PSALM LXXXVII.

THE Church is commended as beloved of God. Neighbouring nations flock to it. It is a spring of refreshing joys.

————————

1. "*His foundation is in the holy mountains.*"

The eye seems to rest on the Temple, the type of God's Church. It stands securely, for it is based on the noble hill of Zion. But what is the stability of the material fabric, compared to that of the spiritual edifice ? Of the former it was said, Not one stone shall be left upon another. The latter is built upon the foundation of prophets and apostles, Jesus Christ Himself being the chief corner-stone. The gates of hell shall not prevail against it.

2. "*The Lord loveth the gates of Zion more than all the dwellings of Jacob.*"

Zion was the spot which the Lord chose and regarded with especial favour. So the Lord loves the Church, and every member of it. Happy the man who can realize, He loved me and gave Himself for me. He hath loved me with an everlasting love: therefore with loving-kindness He hath drawn me. The response follows, I love Him because He first loved me. May our souls ever bathe in the ocean of Christ's unfathomable love !

3. *"Glorious things are spoken of Thee, O city of God."*

No eloquence can sufficiently commend the Church. What can be added to the assurance that she is recognized as the Bride, the Lamb's Wife? She was beloved by the Heavenly Bridegroom before time began, with a love which cannot know a change. She is endowed by Him with all He has, and with all He is. He has placed all the promises as a treasure in her hands. His angels watch around her. His providences guide and defend her path. His righteousness is her beauteous robe, rendering her fit to shine for ever in the palace of the heavenly King. Her seat is prepared beside Him on His throne. It would exhaust all time to give a brief survey of the glories which adorn her.

4, 5, 6. *"I will make mention of Rahab and Babylon to them that know me: behold Philistia, and Tyre, with Ethiopia; this man was born there. And of Zion it shall be said, This and that man was born in her; and the Highest Himself shall establish her. The Lord shall count, when He writeth up the people, that this man was born there."*

The influx of Gentile converts to the Church is here predicted. They shall come from countries which had been noted for their hostility. The Lord shall send forth His mighty Spirit. He shall soften their hearts and open their eyes, and enlighten their understanding, and lead them as willing captives to receive the Gospel yoke. They shall spring up as among the grass, as willows by the water-courses. One shall say, I am the Lord's; another shall call himself by the name of Jacob, and shall surname himself by the name of Israel. And when at last the Book of Life is opened, it shall be found that multitudes from all climes have been gathered into the Church of the living God.

7. "*As well the singers as the players on instruments shall be there : all my springs are in thee.*"

Joy and gladness shall be in her midst. She shall come to the Lord with thanksgiving, and the voice of melody. No element of happiness shall be absent. The Lord's presence near—His presence for evermore—shall be her inexhaustible ocean of delight. Sweetly it is said, In His presence is the fulness of joy: at God's right hand there are pleasures for evermore. Let us now respond, Rejoice in the Lord alway; and again I say, Rejoice. Bless the Lord, O my soul, and all that is within me bless His holy name. Deep and ever fresh are the springs from which we may here draw salvation. Let our tent be always pitched beside this overflowing well. Let us bless His holy name that we have been born again and adopted into the Church of the first-born, whose names are written in heaven. Happy is the present portion: what will be the endless realization!

XVI.

PSALM LXXXVIII.

SOUNDS of bitter grief wail through this Psalm. We hear the mourning of a wounded spirit. All earthly refuge is eschewed; help only is in God.

———————

1, 2. *" O Lord God of my salvation, I have cried day and night before Thee. Let my prayer come before Thee : incline Thine ear unto my cry."*

This Psalm is received as the wailing of Heman the son of Zerah. He was illustrious among men for mental gifts. Solomon scarcely exceeded him in wisdom. But under sense of sin he found not relief in intellect. He flies to God, and pours out his heart in prayer. The whole strain is misery at its full. There is but one word of comfort. He calls upon God, as the God of his salvation. Grasping the plank of saving grace, he could not sink. Let us learn the happy art of wrestling with God, in like spirit of supporting faith.

3, 4, 5. *" For my soul is full of troubles, and my life draweth nigh unto the grave. I am counted with them that go down into the pit : I am as a man that hath no strength. Free among the dead, like the slain that lie in the grave, whom Thou rememberest no more : and they are cut off from Thy hand."*

His soul is faint through excess of anguish. All vital power seems to be extinct. He regards himself as utterly cut off from life, and as now mouldering in the grave. So terrible was his grief that he speaks of himself as already an inmate of the tomb.

6, 7. *" Thou hast laid me in the lowest pit, in darkness, in the deeps. Thy wrath lieth hard upon me, and Thou hast afflicted me with all Thy waves."*

Misery sighs in deeper notes. He mourns as now separated from God. He wails as though lying in the very pit—amid all blackness of darkness—in the uttermost depths. Can misery be more miserable! Let us look up to Jesus. He has delivered us from all wrath.

8, 9. *" Thou hast put away mine acquaintance far from me ; Thou hast made me an abomination unto them : I am shut up, and I cannot come forth. Mine eye mourneth by reason of affliction: Lord, I have called daily upon Thee; I have stretched out my hands unto Thee."*

Troubles lose much of their burden, when loving friends are near to solace. This comfort was denied to Heman. Alone he mourned. Such too was the lonely state of our beloved Lord. All His friends forsook Him and fled. Prayer will bring Jesus to our side. We may plead His promise, I will never leave Thee, nor forsake Thee.

10, 11, 12. *" Wilt Thou show wonders to the dead ? shall the dead arise and praise Thee ? Shall Thy loving-kindness be declared in the grave ? or Thy faithfulness in destruction ? Shall thy wonders be known in the dark ? and Thy righteousness in the land of forgetfulness ? "*

The plea is urged, that relief delayed may be too late. When we lie down in the grave, we can no more show forth God's praise, or spread abroad His wonders. While life continues, let us strive to magnify Him, before all our powers are silent in the grave.

13, 14. *" But unto Thee have I cried, O Lord ; and in the morning shall my prayer prevent Thee. Lord, why castest Thou off my soul ? Why hidest Thou Thy face from me ? "*

While we have life let it be prayer. This grace will prevail. Let the earliest dawn witness our supplications. Let our cry be the first utterance which reaches God. Let us thus seek to learn why He is absent from us, and why His smile no longer cheers.

15, 16, 17, 18. *" I am afflicted and ready to die from my youth up : while I suffer Thy terrors I am distracted. Thy fierce wrath goeth over me ; Thy terrors have cut me off. They came round about me daily like water ; they compassed me about together. Lover and friend hast Thou put far from me, and mine acquaintance into darkness."*

Fearful is this picture of a soul agonizing under a sense of God's withdrawal. What must be the misery of those realms, into which hope never comes! Let us strive to look off from sin's deserts, to the boundless merits of the dying Saviour. He verily redeems from all iniquity. He is the Lamb of God that taketh away the sin of the world. Let us flee to Him. Let us cling to Him. Let us rejoice in Him. Sheltered in Him we cannot be exposed to wrath. There is redemption through His blood, even the forgiveness of our sins. O Jesu! we bless Thee, we adore Thee!

XVII.

PSALM LXXXIX. 1—23.

THIS Psalm is bright in praises for the countless
mercies of our God, especially for faithfulness to His
covenants. Prayer is added. May we with joyful
hearts adopt this tone!

1, 2. *" I will sing of the mercies of the Lord for ever:
with my mouth will I make known Thy faithfulness to all
generations. For I have said, Mercy shall be built up for
ever: Thy faithfulness shalt Thou establish in the very
heavens."*

Mercy is a theme for everlasting praise. Faithfulness cannot be adequately commended. Mercy and
truth go hand in hand to consummate salvation.
Mercy and truth shall ever be the song of the redeemed.
May they be our song now!

3, 4. *" I have made a covenant with my chosen, I have
sworn unto David my servant. Thy seed will I establish
for ever, and build up thy throne to all generations."*

We have here the glad announcement that a covenant
is established by God with Jesus the Son of David.
This covenant secures the perpetuity of the chosen
seed. It stands for ever.

5, 6. *" And the heavens shall praise Thy wonders, O
Lord; Thy faithfulness also in the congregation of the
saints. For who in the heaven can be compared unto the*

Lord? who among the sons of the mighty can be likened unto the Lord?"

Due praise awaits the Lord for these His wonders. It shall commence on earth. It shall be lengthened throughout the days of heaven. These wonders are great beyond all thought. They spring from the unchanging heart of Him, who is the great I AM.

7, 8, 9, 10. *"God is greatly to be feared in the assembly of the saints, and to be had in reverence of all them that are about Him. O Lord God of hosts, who is a strong Lord like unto Thee? or to Thy faithfulness round about Thee? Thou rulest the raging of the sea: when the waves thereof arise, Thou stillest them. Thou hast broken Rahab in pieces, as one that is slain: Thou hast scattered Thine enemies with Thy strong arm."*

Should not filial fear, and holy reverence encircle the throne of God! Mark His might. Is the earth full of commotion? If He speaks, stillness reigns. If He displays His power, His enemies vanish, as smoke before the wind.

11, 12, 13, 14. *"The heavens are Thine, the earth, also is Thine: as for the world and the fulness thereof Thou hast founded them. The north and the south Thou hast created them: Tabor and Hermon shall rejoice in Thy name. Thou hast a mighty arm: strong is Thy hand, and high is Thy right hand. Justice and judgment are the habitation of Thy throne: mercy and truth shall go before Thy face."*

Survey the universe. It is the work of His hands. From north to south creation recognises Him as sovereign Lord. Thus great is His power. Great, too, are all His attributes. Justice and judgment are His abode. Mercy and truth precede His steps.

15, 16, 17, 18. " *Blessed is the people that know the joyful sound ; they shall walk, O Lord, in the light of Thy countenance. In Thy name shall they rejoice all the day : and in Thy righteousness shall they be exalted. For Thou art the glory of their strength ; and in Thy favour our horn shall be exalted. For the Lord is our defence ; and the Holy One of Israel is our King.*"

Blessed indeed are they whose ears receive the gospel's joyful sound. Their walk is bright, for God shines on them. In His Name and in His righteousness they are exalted. He is the glory of their strength. In Him security surrounds them.

19, 20, 21, 22, 23. " *Then Thou spakest in vision to thy Holy One, and saidst, I have laid help upon one that is mighty ; I have exalted one chosen out of the people. I have found David My servant ; with My holy oil have I anointed him. With whom My hand shall be established ; Mine arm also shall strengthen him. The enemy shall not exact upon him ; nor the son of wickedness afflict him. And I will beat down his foes before his face, and plague them that hate him.*"

Here Jesus is most gloriously revealed. He is called of God to be out uttermost salvation. He is anointed as our Prophet, Priest, and King. No enemy shall prevail against Him. May we receive Him in all His offices, and powers, and work, and thus be seated on the pinnacle of safety.

XVIII,

PSALM LXXXIX. 24–52.

24, 25, 26, 27, 28, 29. *" But My faithfulness and My mercy shall be with him ; and in My Name shall his horn be exalted. I will set his hand also in the sea, and his right hand in the rivers. He shall cry unto Me, Thou art my Father, my God, and the Rock of my salvation. Also I will make him my firstborn, higher than the kings of the earth. My mercy will I keep for him for evermore, and My covenant shall stand fast with him. His seed also will I make to endure for ever, and his throne as the days of heaven."*

It is the delight of faith to contemplate Jesus thus exalted by Jehovah's power to the throne of salvation. The Father proclaims Him, Thou art My Son, this day have I begotten Thee. His voice responds, Thou art My Father, My God, and the Rock of My salvation. The promise goes forth, I will make His seed to endure for ever. Eternal glory shall be the sure property of all who believe in Him. Shall we not laud Him with all the faculties that we possess ; and trust Him at every moment of our time !

30, 31, 32, 33, 34, 35, 36, 37. *" If his children forsake My law, and walk not in My judgments ; If they break My statutes, and keep not My commandments ; Then will I visit their transgression with the rod, and their iniquity with stripes. Nevertheless my loving-kindness will I not utterly take from him, nor suffer My faithfulness to fail. My covenant will I not break, nor alter the thing that is*

gone out of My lips.   Once have I sworn by My holiness,
that I will not lie unto David.   His seed shall endure
for ever, and his throne as the sun before Me.   It shall be
established for ever as the moon, and as a faithful witness
in heaven."

It is sadly foreseen, that His children will ofttimes be transgressors, and stray from gospel-paths.
God will mark their iniquities, and due chastisement
shall recall them to His ways.   But still their rejection
shall not be final.   Loving-kindness will not expire.
The covenant shall abide secure.   Jehovah's oath shall
not be broken.   Not one of Christ's seed shall perish.
His throne shall never totter.   It shall abide, as the
moon in the firmament.   It shall appear as the rain-
bow, the pledge that no deluge shall return.

38, 39, 40, 41, 42, 43, 44, 45. *" But Thou hast cast*
off and abhorred, Thou hast been wroth with Thine
anointed.   Thou hast made void the covenant of Thy
servant ; Thou hast profaned his crown by casting it to
the ground.   Thou hast broken down all his hedges ; Thou
hast brought his strongholds to ruin.   All that pass by
the way spoil him : he is a reproach to his neighbours.
Thou hast set up the right hand of his adversaries ; Thou
hast made all his enemies to rejoice.   Thou hast also
turned the edge of his sword, and hast not made him to
stand in the battle.   Thou hast made his glory to cease,
and cast his throne down to the ground.   The days of his
youth hast Thou shortened : Thou hast covered him with
shame."

The scene is here changed.   To all appearance
David's kingdom is brought very low.   His enemies
are allowed to triumph.   His days are shortened,

and shame covers the land. All things indicate desertion. Such is the case in the spiritual kingdom. But
though sins may bring dark days, the sun still rules in
heaven. The covenant may not screen from temporal
distress, but it secures eternal life.

46, 47, 48, 49, 50, 51, 52. "*How long, Lord? wilt
Thou hide Thyself for ever? shall Thy wrath burn like
fire? Remember how short my time is: wherefore hast
Thou made all men in vain? What man is he that
liveth, and shall not see death? shall he deliver his soul
from the hand of the grave? Lord, where are Thy former loving-kindnesses, which Thou swarest unto David in
Thy truth? Remember, Lord, the reproach of Thy servants; how I do bear in my bosom the reproach of all the
mighty people; Wherewith Thine enemies have reproached,
O Lord; wherewith they have reproached the footsteps of
Thine anointed. Blessed be the Lord for evermore. Amen,
and Amen.*"

Faith has undying root in the believer's heart. Cast
down, it is not cast off. It can still send forth the voice
of prayer. It can still call God to look down graciously. It can implore that sufferings may be pitied,
and cruelty rebuked. Deliverance thus sought will be
vouchsafed. The mercies of the covenant stand as a
rock, and the rejoicing spirit will soon shout, Blessed be
the Lord for evermore! Amen and Amen.

XIX.

PSALM XC.

This Psalm is entitled " A Prayer of Moses, the man of God." As such it justly claims devout attention as the earliest of inspired songs. In adopting it may we move forward on the heavenward road !

---

1. " *Lord, Thou hast been our dwelling place in all generations.*"

Happy has been the experience of the saints of God at every period. They could always find a home on high, in which they might repose and sweetly dwell. To all who approach in the name of Jesus the portals of heaven open, and smiles welcome. By faith may we thus enter, and in God continually abide. No monarch occupies so grand a palace.

2. " *Before the mountains were brought forth, or ever Thou hadst formed the earth and the world, even from everlasting to everlasting Thou art God.*"

A glorious description of the self-existent and ever-lasting God here meets us. Before time was, while time rolls on, when time shall be no more, He lives the great " I am that I am."

3, 4, 5, 6. " *Thou turnest man to destruction; and sayest, Return, ye children of men. For a thousand years in Thy sight are but as yesterday when it is past, and as a watch in the night. Thou carriest them away as with*

*a flood ; they are as a sleep: in the morning they are like
grass which groweth up. In the morning it flourisheth,
and groweth up; in the evening it is cut down, and
withereth."*

In contrast mark the short-lived instability of man.
Formed of the dust of the earth, God speaks the word,
and to that dust he instantly returns. In God's sight
time has no place. A thousand years are but as a
fleeting day. Many images combine to show the brevity
of man's existence. A rushing torrent bears him out of
sight. Sleep soon ceases, and in the morning leaves no
trace. The night-watch tarries not. When day dawns
the grass is green, before evening it is withered up.
Human life is but a momentary bloom.

*7, 8, 9. " For we are consumed by Thine anger, and by
Thy wrath are we troubled. Thou hast set our iniquities
before Thee, our secret sins in the light of Thy countenance. For all our days are passed away in Thy wrath ;
we spend our years as a tale that is told."*

Sin is the root of this nothingness. Our iniquities
are many. They may be hid from our view ; but they
are all patent to the omniscience of God. When His
anger is aroused, we vanish as the remembrance of a
brief recital.

*10. " The days of our years are threescore years and ten ;
and if by reason of strength they be fourscore years, yet is
their strength labour and sorrow: for it is soon cut off,
and we fly away."*

They who are permitted to count threescore years
and ten, should regard their allotted course as fully run.
The fleeting generations in the wilderness taught this
lesson to Moses. Few who entered Canaan had seen

that period. If unusual strength should lengthen out
man's days, the failing powers bring labour and sorrow.
The continuance is evanescent. Departure is at the
door.

11, 12. " *Who knoweth the power of Thine anger?
even according to Thy fear so is Thy wrath. So teach us
to number our days, that we may apply our hearts unto
wisdom.*"

God is not limited in any attribute. His anger then
may work terribly. Let us tremble to provoke His
wrath: and rather in knowledge of life's brevity give
our little space to search for true wisdom. He is well
taught who studies God in Christ.

13, 14, 15, 16, 17. " *Return, O Lord, how long? and
let it repent Thee concerning Thy servants. O satisfy us
early with Thy mercy; that we may rejoice and be glad
all our days. Make us glad according to the days wherein
Thou hast afflicted us, and the years wherein we have seen
evil. Let Thy work appear unto Thy servants, and Thy
glory unto their children. And let the beauty of the Lord
our God be upon us: and establish Thou the work of our
hands upon us; yea, the work of our hands establish
Thou it.*"

Solemn prayers are the fitting conclusion. The Lord
is implored to return, to relax displeasure, to cause
mercy to overflow. Then joy and gladness will superabound. He will not be slow to reveal His wondrous
power to beautify His people with salvation, and to
make all their work to prosper. May these prayers
ever ascend from our hearts! Descending blessings will
crown us with delights.

XX.

PSALM XCI.

INTERNAL evidence establishes that the apprehension of near sickness and the approach of pestilence awakened this Psalm. Firm confidence is expressed in God's protecting power. May we find Him a very present help in all our troubles!

1. " *He that dwelleth in the secret place of the Most High shall abide under the shadow of the Almighty.*"

The Ark behind the veil was regarded as the symbol of God's presence. Common gaze penetrates not the secret place. In general men strive not for acquaintedness with God. They seek Him not in Christ. But they who thus find Him will ever cling to Him with strengthening grasp. They will rest in Him as in a calm and cool abode. His shadow will ward off the fiery darts of Satan, and avert the hot persecution of the ungodly.

2. " *I will say of the Lord, He is my refuge and my fortress: my God; in Him will I trust.*"

Faith makes bold profession. It casts off fear, and avows that in God it finds a safe retreat—a sure protection—an almighty friend. This confidence will never be disappointed.

3, 4, 5, 6. " *Surely He shall deliver thee from the snare of the fowler, and from the noisome pestilence. He shall cover thee with His feathers, and under His wings shalt*

*thou trust: His truth shall be thy shield and buckler.
Thou shalt not be afraid for the terror by night; nor for
the arrow that flieth by day; nor for the pestilence that
walketh in darkness; nor for the destruction that wasteth
at noon-day."*

Troubles are enumerated such as are common to this
mortal lot. But trust in God exalts above their fatal reach.
The fowler may lay hidden snares, but they shall not
entrap. The noisome pestilence shall inflict no death-
ful wound. The Almighty shall extend His covering
wing. His faithful promises shall uphold the combatant
in the hour of battle. By night, by day, the dwelling
shall be impervious to plague. There may be a literal
reference to the deliverance of Israel's sons, and their
exemption from all contact with harm when plagues
laid low the Egyptian hosts. There may be spiritual
reference to the deliverance of God's children from the
destroying attacks of Satan. But one truth is undeni-
able. The real happiness and safety of true believers
is emphatically assured, and we are exhorted to pray
for sustaining faith, and in all perils to trust without
one fear.

7, 8, 9, 10. *" A thousand shall fall at thy side, and ten
thousand at thy right hand; but it shall not come nigh
thee. Only with thine eyes shalt thou behold and see the
reward of the wicked. Because thou hast made the Lord,
which is my refuge, even the Most High, thy habitation;
there shall no evil befall thee, neither shall any plague come
nigh thy dwelling."*

Other terms are added to strengthen assurance.
They who by faith repose on God shall surely be
upheld. Though troubles be multiplied, they shall

never be cast off. In much seeming peril they shall be really safe.

11, 12. *" For He shall give His angels charge over Thee, to keep Thee in all Thy ways. They shall bear Thee up in their hands, lest Thou dash Thy foot against a stone."*

This promise is distinctly addressed to Jesus. As such the devil quoted it, and Jesus heard without rejection. If we are one with Jesus, the promises which were poured upon His head will flow down to us, and will invest us in security.

13, 14, 15, 16. *" Thou shalt tread upon the lion and adder; the young lion and the dragon shalt thou trample under feet. Because He hath set His love upon Me, therefore will I deliver him: I will set him on high, because he hath known My name. He shall call upon Me, and I will answer him: I will be with him in trouble; I will deliver him, and honour him. With long life will I satisfy him, and show him My salvation."*

The same encouraging strain still sounds. All who have set their love on God, and all who know His name, may claim fulfilment. They shall have deliverance in every day of trouble. God will honour them in time, and honour them with a long life, even for ever and ever. Happy indeed are the people who thus dwell in the secret place of the Most High.

XXI.

PSALM XCII.

HERE strong exhortations enforce the duty of praise. Motives for such adoration are specified. May they tune our hearts to luxuriate in like pastures of joy!

———————

1, 2, 3. "*It is a good thing to give thanks unto the Lord, and to sing praises unto Thy name, O Most High: to show forth Thy loving-kindness in the morning, and Thy faithfulness every night, upon an instrument of ten strings, and upon the psaltery ; upon the harp with a solemn sound.*"

Thanksgiving raises the heart above this lower scene. It is the melody which sounds in heaven. It should be the happiness of earth. Our mercies are boundless and unmerited. For each warm praise should be uplifted. But here our powers flag. Let us pray that the Spirit may revive and strengthen them. Let gratitude to God brighten the dawn of day. Let the last sounds of evening bear testimony to His faithfulness. Thus let each day declare that loving and faithful is the Lord. Every faculty and every means of harmony should be summoned to give aid to heaven-taught praise.

4. "*For Thou, Lord, hast made me glad through Thy work ; I will triumph in the works of Thy hands.*"

A mighty motive impels the believer's heart. It is experience of God's wondrous dealings. Marvels of love are shown in creation, providence, and grace. The believer knows that all things work together for his good. He doubts not that goodness and mercy will follow him all the days of his life; that victory over all foes and impediments is before him; and that at last he shall reign in triumph. Can he realize these truths and not exult in praises?

5, 6, 7, 8, 9. "*O Lord, how great are Thy works! and Thy thoughts are very deep. A brutish man knoweth not; neither doth a fool understand this. When the wicked spring as the grass, and when all the workers of iniquity do flourish; it is that they shall be destroyed for ever. But Thou, Lord, art most high for evermore. For, lo, Thine enemies, O Lord, for, lo, Thine enemies shall perish; all the workers of iniquity shall be scattered.*"

Ignorance of God's power involves the world in darkness. The ungodly show a flourishing appearance. They spring up in multitudes. But their prosperity is short-lived. God speaks and nothingness becomes their grave. All who oppose Him have a fruitless toil. They labour only to insure destruction.

10, 11. "*But my horn shalt Thou exalt like the horn of an unicorn: I shall be anointed with fresh oil. Mine eye also shall see my desire on mine enemies; and mine ears shall hear my desire of the wicked that rise up against me.*"

The ungodly will surely perish. So surely will the godly triumph. Mighty strength shall be supplied, which shall level mountains of hindrances. Joy and gladness shall be their portion. They shall receive the unction of the Holy One. Where are their foes? They are brought low. What sound reaches the ear? It is the wailing of hopeless discomfiture.

12, 13, 14, 15. " *The righteous shall flourish like the palm-tree; he shall grow like a cedar in Lebanon. Those that be planted in the house of the Lord shall flourish in the courts of our God. They shall still bring forth fruit in old age; they shall be fat and flourishing; to show that the Lord is upright: He is my rock, and there is no unrighteousness in Him.*"

Images of verdure and fertility depict the beauteous prosperity of the righteous. We learn too in what soil they are rooted. They are planted in the house of the Lord. They live in heavenly fellowship. They realize God's presence. They delight in His ordinances. Their fruitfulness is that of the choicest trees. Their last days shall be their best. Their works of age shall exceed those of youth. This assurance comes from the character of their God. Like the rock, He cannot be moved; and His uprightness ratifies His word. Security promised is security enjoyed.

XXII.

PSALM XCIII.

THE reign of Christ here shines forth in illustrious splendour. It is glorious in power and holiness. May the description lead our hearts to more intense desire to serve devotedly our heavenly King!

---

1. "*The Lord reigneth; He is clothed with majesty; the Lord is clothed with strength, wherewith He hath girded Himself: the world also is stablished, that it cannot be moved.*"

Jesus is proclaimed as King. What confidence, what peace should this assurance give! He reigns supreme. All power is given unto Him in heaven and in earth. His kingdom ruleth over all. Irresistible is His sway. Nothing can thwart His sovereign will. He directs all things in providence and grace, in time and in eternity. He appears in His royal robes of majesty and glory. Let us meekly bend the knee, and give the homage due to His supremacy. He wears the girdle of omnipotence. Let us delight in the thought. It proclaims the security of those who seek the shelter of His wings. The earth is the present scene of their abode, and no power can shake its stability. It rests on firmness and cannot be moved.

2. "*Thy throne is established of old; Thou art from everlasting.*"

Earthly kingdoms quickly rise and fall. Yesterday they were not; to-morrow they are gone. A breath makes them, and a breath destroys. But eternity is the possession of this King. Before time was, He lived " I AM." When time shall be no more, He still shall be the great " I AM."

3, 4. " *The floods have lifted up, O Lord, the floods have lifted up their voice; the floods lift up their waves. The Lord on high is mightier than the noise of many waters, yea, than the mighty waves of the sea.*"

Though Jesus is thus mighty, He reigns not unopposed. Wild and frantic passions are in commotion against Him. Mark the sea when raging tempests lash its billows into fury. Terribly they swell. Gigantic waves uplift their foaming heads. They dash against the rocks, as if their strength could overcome all barriers. But in vain they toss and swell. Thus the maddened rage of rebel man is weak against this kingdom. Christ sits above the water floods. He calmly views the impotent infatuation. Happy are they who are for ever one with Him. They too shall sit on thrones.

5. " *Thy testimonies are very sure: holiness becometh Thine house, O Lord, for ever.*"

Repeated testimonies announce with trumpet-tongue this truth. The Word abounds with declarations that the government is upon Christ's shoulder. This Word cannot be broken. His empire must abide for ever. Sweet is the concluding word. His right hand is full of righteousness. The sceptre of His kingdom is a right sceptre. All His rule is holy. Holiness is inscribed on all His work, ordinances, and decrees. His people, too, are all holy. Holiness is the bright title on their brow.

May we be holy even as our Lord is holy! May our constant prayer be, Sanctify us wholly, body, soul, and spirit! Sanctify us through Thy truth! Thus alone can we take comfort in the hope of gazing for ever on the unclouded glory of our God. Heaven is holiness in more than meridian splendour. The entrance of evil in the slightest form would change the total aspect. Light could not be one with darkness. The torrid zone could not show icy plains. The door is barred against iniquity. The Lamb's bride is all-glorious without in the pure obedience of the Lord, and all-glorious within through the indwelling of the Spirit.

XXIII.

PSALM XCIV.

GOD is supplicated to maintain His cause and not to
allow His enemies to triumph. Afflictions are named
as frequent benefits, and the afflicted are assured of
comfort. May this hymn teach and console!

———————

1, 2. "*O Lord God, to whom vengeance belongeth; O
God, to whom vengeance belongeth, show Thyself. Lift up
Thyself, Thou Judge of the earth; render a reward to the
proud.*"

Faith knows that it may boldly call upon God to
manifest His rebuking powers. It desires that evil may
cease. It knows that if God should arise, this issue
would quickly be accomplished, and the proud lie low
in shame.

3, 4, 5, 6, 7. "*Lord, how long shall the wicked, how
long shall the wicked triumph? How long shall they
utter and speak hard things? and all the workers of
iniquity boast themselves? They break in pieces Thy
people, O Lord, and afflict thine heritage: They slay the
widow and the stranger, and murder the fatherless. Yet
they say, the Lord shall not see, neither shall the God of
Jacob regard it.*"

Cries for God's interference are redoubled. The
cruelty of the ungodly seems to prevail too long.

Various acts of their tyranny and oppression are enumerated. The godly know that help only can come from heaven. Thus supplications are multiplied.

8, 9, 10. " *Understand, ye brutish among the people: and ye fools, when will ye be wise? He that planted the ear, shall He not hear? He that formed the eye, shall He not see? He that chastiseth the heathen, shall not He correct? He that teacheth man knowledge, shall not He know?*"

Remonstrance is addressed to the ungodly. They are rebuked for their presumption. They are reminded of the power and omniscience of God. He who endows man with organs of intelligence, shall He not be intelligent? Shall He from whom all knowledge comes, lack knowledge? Omniscience is His attribute. No evil can escape detection. The hand of punishment will work vengeance.

11, 12, 13. " *The Lord knoweth the thoughts of man, that they are vanity. Blessed is the man whom Thou chastenest, O Lord, and teachest him out of Thy law; that Thou mayest give him rest from the days of adversity, until the pit be digged for the wicked.*"

Vain man may plot iniquity. But he sows the wind to reap the whirlwind. Afflictions may thus be heaped on the righteous; but they will prove to be real mercies. They often are blessings in disguise. They will drive to the study of God's Word. Thus the blessed man will find delight and profit in the contemplations of God's law. And yet a little while he will see that the ungodly have fought against themselves.

14, 15, 16. " *For the Lord will not cast off His people, neither will He forsake His inheritance: but judgment shall return unto righteousness; and all the upright in heart shall follow it. Who will rise up for me against the evil-doers? or who will stand up for me against the workers of iniquity?"*

For ever is the grand truth established in heaven, I will never leave thee nor forsake thee. The Lord hateth putting away. With Him is no variableness, neither shadow of turning. His sheep shall never perish, neither shall any pluck them out of His hand. In all our trials let us trust and not be afraid.

17, 18, 19, 20, 21, 22, 23. *"Unless the Lord had been my help, my soul had almost dwelt in silence. When I said, My foot slippeth; Thy mercy, O Lord, held me up. In the multitude of my thoughts within me Thy comforts delight my soul. Shall the throne of iniquity have fellowship with Thee, which frameth mischief by a law? They gather themselves together against the soul of the righteous, and condemn the innocent blood. But the Lord is my defence; and my God is the rock of my refuge. And He shall bring upon them their own iniquity, and shall cut them off in their own wickedness; yea, the Lord our God shall cut them off."*

If God could desert, the godly must perish. But this can never be, and therefore they live and prosper. And in all the misgivings of their troubled minds God's comforts are their stay. There is an awful contrast. God will arise, and uttermost perdition will overwhelm all wickedness.

XXIV.

PSALM XCV.

WARM exhortations call to joyful thanksgivings. It is shown that God is truly entitled to such homage. Warnings to the unbelieving and disobedient are adjoined. May the life-giving Spirit teach us!

1, 2. "*O come, let us sing unto the Lord; let us make a joyful noise to the Rock of our salvation. Let us come before His presence with thanksgiving, and make a joyful noise unto Him with psalms.*"

It is good to encourage each other in every holy work, especially in the work of encircling our God with praises. Abundant causes awaken thanksgivings. He is the strength of our salvation. Who can estimate what salvation is? It is decreed in the counsels of the Triune Jehovah. It is wrought out by the great God and our Saviour Jesus Christ. It is applied by the great God the Holy Ghost. Let us therefore gladly hasten into His presence and throng His courts. Let us be loud and fervent in acclamations of delight. Salvation is a rock raised and supported by Jehovah.

3, 4, 5. "*For the Lord is a great God, and a great King above all gods. In His hand are the deep places of the earth; the strength of the hills is His also. The sea is His, and He made it; and His hands formed the dry land.*"

Consider the mighty motives which kindle our gratitude. Ponder God's majesty and greatness. Potentates of earth vanish before Him. Their power is utter weakness. He is invested with all supremacy as King of kings and Lord of lords. Mark creation's multitudinous fabric. He spake the word, and the world assumed existence. All things in land and sea own His sway. Great are these wonders. He is Lord, whose will created and maintains the universal frame of nature.

6, 7. " O come, let us worship and bow down; let us kneel before the Lord our Maker. For He is our God, and we are the people of His pasture, and the sheep of His hand."

Such contemplation should prostrate us before His throne. We are also especially led to worship when we consider His inestimable goodness. He is the tender Shepherd. We are the flock of His watchful care. He leads us to lie down in the green pastures of His truth. He guides us to drink the still waters of His refreshing love. Let us then in deep humility adore.

8, 9, 10, 11. " To-day if ye will hear His voice, harden not your heart, as in the provocation, and as in the day of temptation in the wilderness, when your fathers tempted Me, proved Me, and saw My work. Forty years long was I grieved with this generation, and said, It is a people that do err in their heart, and they have not known My ways: unto whom I sware in My wrath, that they should not enter into My rest."

Let there be no delay. To-day Jehovah calls us. To-morrow our ears may be incapable to hear. Let us use every means to melt and soften our obdurate hearts. If they are hardened, we shall love error and hate truth.

The case of the children of Israel gives awful warning.
We know how they tempted and provoked their God.
We know how His word went forth that they should not
enter into the rest of the promised land. The home of
faith is open to us, where we may calmly rest from all
our works. The rest of heaven is also promised. By
faith may we now rest in Christ, and pass from this
present rest to the eternal rest of heaven. We marvel
at the mad rebellion of Israel's sons. We condemn
their hearts as harder than the nether millstone. It
seems incredible that through their long pilgrimage
they would not see the leading hand of God. While
we blame them, let us look inward. If we should similarly err, can we escape their doom !

XXV.

PSALM XCVI.

AGAIN we are loudly called to magnify the Lord in joyful song. Thoughts are directed to the extension of Christ's kingdom. He is proclaimed as coming to consummate salvation. May our souls respond, "Come, Lord Jesus, come quickly!"

———————

1, 2, 3. "*O sing unto the Lord a new song; sing unto the Lord, all the earth. Sing unto the Lord, bless His name; show forth His salvation from day to day. Declare His glory among the heathen, His wonders among all people.*"

Praise never can be too exuberant. Everything that hath breath should live to praise the Lord. In this work there never should be weariness. Causes of praise are ever fresh, and fresh should be the responding notes. Let us sing a new song. New thoughts, new motives should enliven the soul. Our hearts should ever seek renewal, and be looking onward to the new heavens and the new earth, where He shall reign who hath made all things new. Hence new should be our song. As day succeeds to day, so let praise succeed to praise. Let too our diligent efforts convey to the poor and ignorant of every clime the tidings of redeeming love. Let the heathen learn through us the glories of Christ's salvation.

4, 5, 6. "*For the Lord is great, and greatly to be praised: He is to be feared above all gods. For all the gods of the nations are idols: but the Lord made the heavens. Honour and majesty are before Him; strength and beauty are in His sanctuary.*"

Behold the greatness, the supremacy, the glory of our God. Heathen idols are utter vanity. Let us call the poor heathen to cease to bow down to stocks and stones. Let us teach them to worship Him who hath made heaven and earth. This worship is mighty to enliven and sanctify. It is beautified with all the radiancy of heaven's glory.

7, 8, 9. "*Give unto the Lord, O ye kindreds of the people, give unto the Lord glory and strength. Give unto the Lord the glory due unto His name: bring an offering, and come into His courts. O worship the Lord in the beauty of holiness; fear before Him, all the earth.*"

Who can describe the pure delight of spiritual worship! Let us draw near to Him who is a Spirit in spirit and in truth. Let it be our choice joy to magnify His holy name, to ascribe unto Him the glory which is so greatly His, and to acknowledge the omnipotence with which He is invested. Let it be our delight to consecrate to Him all the resources with which we are endowed; to present unto Him ourselves, our bodies, souls, and spirits, which are His by every right of creation, redemption, conquest, and our own surrender. Let us reverently seek His hallowed courts, and offer holy service. There is no beauty to be compared with holiness, which is the reflection of our God.

10, 11, 12, 13. "*Say among the heathen, that the Lord reigneth: the world also shall be established that it shall not be moved : He shall judge the people righteously.   Let the heavens rejoice, and let the earth be glad ; let the sea roar, and the fulness thereof.   Let the field be joyful, and all that is therein : then shall all the trees of the wood rejoice before the Lord ; for He cometh, for He cometh to judge the earth : He shall judge the world with righteousness, and the people with His truth."*

Nothing quickens praise more than constant expectation of the coming of the Lord.   Yet a little while and He that shall come will come and will not tarry.   Behold He cometh leaping upon the mountains and skipping upon the hills.   Oh thrice blessed, thrice glorious day! The heavens and the earth, with their ten thousand tongues, shall rejoice and sing.   Righteous shall be His reign.   Truth shall be exalted, and the tabernacle of God shall be with men.   Should not this prospect warm our hearts to spread abroad His glorious name!   Surely the very stones would rebuke our silence.

XXVI.

PSALM XCVII.

FAITH is encouraged to joyful contemplation of Christ's kingdom. It may be hidden from the world; but it is terrible to all adversaries. Exhortations follow to abound in holy joy.

---

1. "*The Lord reigneth; let the earth rejoice; let the multitude of isles be glad thereof.*"

The Lord reigneth. This is the Gospel's note. It is a truth prolific of holy joy. All events obey His sceptre. In every circumstance, therefore, joy should wave its tranquil wand throughout the heart. Every occurrence should whisper, It is the Lord: let Him do what seemeth Him good. Events may sometimes show a frowning aspect, but happy believers receive them as blessings in foreign guise.

2. "*Clouds and darkness are round about Him: righteousness and judgment are the habitation of His throne.*"

Faith may not always discern the purport of God's rule. To the ungodly His will is shrouded in impenetrable darkness. They know not the mighty Ruler. They understand not the workings of His hand. Solemn lessons are embodied in the word, If they had known, they would not have crucified the Lord of glory. But His throne is established high on the pinnacle of righteousness and judgment. All the decrees of His tri-

bunal are offsprings of these attributes, and shine as
reflections of His glory. Happy, indeed, are they in
whose hearts the Lord God reigns righteously.

3, 4, 5, 6. *" A fire goeth before Him, and burneth up
His enemies round about. His lightnings enlightened the
world : the earth saw, and trembled. The hills melted
like wax at the presence of the Lord, at the presence of the
Lord of the whole earth. The heavens declare His righteousness, and all the people see His glory."*

Thoughts here revert to Sinai's terrors. When the
fiery law was promulgated, awful manifestations announced that vengeance would destroy opponents. In
Christ's kingdom, holy indignation is also against all
unrighteousness. Here strong images are employed to
show that wrath will scrutinize and rightly execute its
tremendous work. Tribulation and anguish must be
the rebel's doom. Blessed are they who are delivered
from this wrath, and are translated into the kingdom of
God's dear Son.

7, 8, 9. *" Confounded be all they that serve graven
images, that boast themselves of idols : worship Him, all
ye gods. Zion heard, and was glad ; and the daughters
of Judah rejoiced because of Thy judgments, O Lord. For
Thou, Lord, art high above all the earth : Thou art exalted far above all gods."*

Let no fond dream suggest that idolatry is not an
abomination in God's sight. Truth has denounced its
sure destruction, and destruction will surely come. Let
all who hear take warning, and meekly bow before the
King of kings. The ear of faith hears God's resolve,
and rejoices in the thought that homage and worship
shall be rendered to Him to Whom it is so justly due.

10, 11, 12. " *Ye that love the Lord, hate evil: He pre-serveth the souls of His saints; He delivereth them out of the hand of the wicked. Light is sown for the righteous, and gladness for the upright in heart. Rejoice in the Lord, ye righteous; and give thanks at the remembrance of His holiness.*"

Believers are here pointedly described. Their conspicuous feature is love of their Lord. It is a true address, O Thou Whom my soul loveth! · He demands our hearts. Let them be His in every pulse, at every moment. The best proof of this love will be hatred of all that is adverse to Him. They who love Him will nestle in His heart, and His power will screen them from all harm. As seed sown springs from the bosom of the earth, so light and gladness are laid up for the happy flock, and assuredly will be their portion. They have all cause to rejoice, to be glad, and to give thanks. God's holiness affrights the wicked. The thought is terror to them. His servants ponder this attribute with delight. They turn not from the precept, Be ye holy, for I am holy.

XXVII.

PSALM XCVIII.

EXHORTATIONS to sing praises are here prolonged. Views of Christ's kingdom suggest ample topics. May they kindle holy warmth in our hearts!

----

1. *" O sing unto the Lord a new song ; for He hath done marvellous things : His right hand, and His holy arm, hath gotten Him the victory."*

Praise can never be exhausted. The more we contemplate the exploits of our Lord, the more we are moved to uplift adoration. The lessons of yesterday are expanded by the lessons of to-day. Fresh discoveries awaken new songs. But still no words can fully sing the wondrous works of God. Wonder is inscribed on creation in its every part, and on providence in its perpetual evolutions. But the wonders of redeeming love shine with the brightest blaze. Here Christ appears the mighty conqueror. Hell and its legion had usurped dominion over man. Many chains enthralled him. He was bound in irons of captivity. Jesus undertakes the rescue. He leads captivity captive, and saves His people from the cruel grasp. Alone He does the work. He by Himself purges our sins. Alone He hangs upon the accursed tree. Alone He tramples Satan beneath His feet. To Him be all the praise. In Him salvation triumphs.

2, 3. " *The Lord hath made known His salvation :
His righteousness hath He openly showed in the sight of
the heathen.   He hath remembered His mercy and His
truth toward the house of Israel : all the ends of the
earth have seen the salvation of our God.*"

His glorious victory is proclaimed throughout earth's
length and breadth.   They that dwell in heathen darkness shall hear the wondrous tidings.   All the gracious
promises to Israel's sons shall be abundantly fulfilled.
Is mercy pledged ?   Mercy to the uttermost shall be
vouchsafed.   Every word of eternal truth shall be
established.   Salvation shall be adored, wherever man
draws breath.

4, 5, 6. " *Make a joyful noise unto the Lord, all the
earth : make a loud noise, and rejoice, and sing praise.
Sing unto the Lord with the harp ; with the harp, and
the voice of a psalm.   With trumpets, and sound of
cornet, make a joyful noise before the Lord the King.*"

The claims of the Lord upon resounding praise are
here exhibited in emphatic terms.   When the heart
and affections are thoroughly engaged, every power
will be used.   Not only will the lips be loud in their
utterance, but everything which art can supply and
instruments contribute will be thus hallowed.   Nothing will be withheld, which can with reverence
give aid.

7, 8, 9. " *Let the sea roar, and the fulness thereof ;
the world, and they that dwell therein.   Let the floods
clap their hands : let the hills be joyful together before
the Lord : for He cometh to judge the earth ; with
righteousness shall He judge the world, and the people
with equity.*"

Universal nature is next addressed. Everything which the Lord made should in some sense be hand-maid to His praise. Let us hear in the roaring of the billows the acknowledgment of His Being. Let us see in the forests and the hills evidence of His great-ness. Above all let us praise Him for the glories of His coming kingdom. Blessed be His holy name, He comes, He surely comes, He quickly comes. He shall take unto Himself His great power and reign, and His kingdom shall be righteousness. Then earth will be one wide expanse of universal joy. Nature will put on her renovated dress. The sea in all its amplitude, the earth with all who occupy its space, the floods, the hills, with joyful tongues will swell the triumph. Let us by glad anticipation learn to take our part.

XXVIII.

PSALM XCIX.

ATTENTION is again called to the greatness and glory of
Christ's kingdom. Exhortations to worship Him suit-
ably follow. May the Spirit write them on our hearts!

---

1. "*The Lord reigneth; let the people tremble: He
sitteth between the cherubims; let the earth be moved.*"
The Gospel-note here sounds again. The Holy Spirit
delights to proclaim Jesus seated supreme upon His
throne. This thought is an overflowing cup of joy. It
presents strong consolation. Oh! that He might reign
in us, and make our hearts His chosen home. But with
this comfort awe should be intermixed. We should
tremble lest any rebel passion should dispute His rule.
This fear should keep us lowly in submission. His
high seat too is a throne of grace. It is foreshadowed by
the mercy-seat, over which the cherubims spread their
wings. Let us adore Him as our King. Let the whole
earth be one activity of service.

2, 3. "*The Lord is great in Zion; and He is high
above all the people. Let them praise Thy great and terrible name; for it is holy.*"
The greatness of our King exceeds all thought. His
might is truly omnipotent. His will is irresistible.
Hence His name is terrible, and no foe can stand against
Him. If He speak, opponents crumble into very dust.

But holiness reigns co-equal with His greatness.   He is
holy in working salvation for His people.   He is holy
in executing vengeance on His adversaries.

4, 5. "*The King's strength also loveth judgment : Thou
dost establish equity, Thou executest judgment and righteousness in Jacob.   Exalt ye the Lord our God and worship at His footstool ; for He is holy.*"

Our mighty King, the strength of His people, takes
especial delight in vindicating the cause of the oppressed.
In His kingdom righteous dealings are the rule.   Mighty
motives urge us to fall low before Him, and to adore
Him as the Holy, Holy, Holy Lord God of Hosts.

6, 7. "*Moses and Aaron among His priests, and
Samuel among them that call upon His name ; they
called upon the Lord, and He answered them.   He spake
unto them in the cloudy pillar : they kept His testimonies,
and the ordinance that He gave them.*"

We are encouraged to worship by the example of the
holiest saints of old.   Consider Moses and Aaron.   They
were servants who ministered unto Him.   Regard
Samuel.   His life was consecrated to render service.
It was their delight, too, to pour out their hearts in
prayer.   Did they pray in vain ?   That could not be.
The Lord's ears were ever open to their cry, and ready
answers flew on the wings of love.   He was ever near
to hold communion with them.   Out of the overshadowing cloud His commands were heard, and reverence
hastened to obey.

8, 9. "*Thou answeredst them, O Lord our God : Thou
wast a God that forgavest them, though Thou tookest vengeance of their inventions.   Exalt the Lord our God, and
worship at His holy hill ; for the Lord our God is holy.*"

But still the favoured people were but men. In sin they were conceived. Hence they often started aside as a broken bow. Thus they were brought into grievous straits, and God's displeasure could not be withholden. But still He was a God ready to pardon. Where sin abounded forgiving mercy abounded much more. Can we refrain to adore, to worship, and to praise! We rob our souls of their most hallowed joy when we are slow to revel in this exercise. It is Godlike condescension that His ears are open to our feeble strains of worship. Shall He be willing to accept our worthless tribute, and shall we reluctantly present it? Forbid it, every feeling of our hearts!

XXIX.

PSALM C.

THIS hymn has been, and still is, the delight of Christian hearts. Its pervading note is a call to adoring praise. Praise is due to our God, because of His sovereignty, and His tender care. May praise ever fill our hearts and dwell on our lips!

1, 2. *" Make a joyful noise unto the Lord, all ye lands. Serve the Lord with gladness; come before His presence with singing."*

Throughout the length and breadth of the earth the praises of God should be the joyful sound. The feeling should be mighty in our hearts, and should swell in no feeble strain. It should be our chief joy to render service to the Lord. His people are called to dwell in realms of happiness. Their whole career should give a good report of His gracious dealings. His worship should be their constant pleasure-ground; it should resound with notes of melody and thanksgiving. Eternity will be too short fully to recount His praise. Let us not shorten our joy by neglecting to begin on earth.

3. *" Know ye that the Lord He is God: it is He that hath made us, and not we ourselves: we are His people, and the sheep of His pasture."*

It is good to call others to the knowledge of the

Lord. This is a wondrous theme, and well demands our utmost powers. In the first place we should commend His glorious supremacy. But who can tell His essence as God! His name is opened out to us in His blessed attributes. Each calls us to proclaim Him in varied terms. We live on earth; wondrous is the thought! Whence did we acquire our being? His will called us from nothingness to be living souls. The breath of life is entirely His gift. Let us never forget that we are His by creative power. But we are His for ever by His covenant-engagements. He has chosen us to be His favoured flock. He has selected us to be the sheep of His pasture. It is through His distinguishing grace that we are brought to revel in the rich pastures of Gospel-truth, and to draw water with joy out of the wells of salvation.

4, 5. "*Enter into His gates with thanksgiving, and into His courts with praise: be thankful unto Him, and bless His name. For the Lord is good; His mercy is everlasting; and His truth endureth to all generations.*"

Shall we not then throng His courts with praise, and cause His sanctuary to resound with adorations! Again and again topics of praise abound around us. With joyful lips let us speak of all His goodness. It is unsearchable, unmerited, infinite, everlasting. Let us here begin the testimony which can never end. From age to age His truth shall live; from age to age let joyful lips proclaim it! Amen.

XXX.

PSALM CI.

Rules are prescribed for godly government. Advice is given to those who exercise authority. May all take heed ; for to each some influence belongs.

———————

1, 2. "*I will sing of mercy and judgment : unto Thee, O Lord, will I sing. I will behave myself wisely in a perfect way. O when wilt Thou come unto me ? I will walk within my house with a perfect heart.*"

Praise is the inmate of the godly heart. The Psalmist engages that songs to the Lord shall be his glad employ. Mercy and judgment compose the happy theme. To think of God's mercy is the delight of delights. To utter its praise is the antepast of heaven. Judgment, too, claims its place. The Lord is not slow to vindicate what is the right. His righteous dealings should be magnified continually. But the mercy and the judgment, which are the attributes of the Lord, should also be the characteristics of magisterial rulers. They who are invested with the exercise of authority should realize that they are ordained of God to represent Him. Hence His mode of governing should be their studied pattern. But left to themselves men are poor and ignorant and weak. Every man in his best estate is altogether vanity. Hence our prayer for the teaching and indwelling of the Spirit should be earnest and incessant. Oh, when wilt Thou come unto me? His presence is light and strength and power. It never is denied to those who truly serve and seek Him. He that hath My commandments and keepeth them, he it is that loveth Me. And he that loveth Me shall be loved of My Father, and We will come unto him, and take up Our abode with him. Thus the pious man looks up for heavenly aid, and resolves that he will act with wisdom and discretion. He will diligently watch that no flaw shall stain his godly walk. His heart shall be wholly given to the Lord : and the heart is the rudder of all conduct.

3. " *I will set no wicked thing before mine eyes: I hate the work of them that turn aside; it shall not cleave to me.*"

He will guard the portal of every sense. If evil is before him, he will close his eyes, lest some pollution should gain entrance. He will utterly abhor the works of those who deviate from the path of piety. Their work shall be shunned with disgust.

4. " *A froward heart shall depart from me : I will not know a wicked person.*"

The world abounds with self-willed and perverse rebels. They submit to no righteous rule. These shall be banished from the sight of the righteous. No wicked man shall be among their friends. Their joy shall be in the select company of the godly.

5, 6, 7, 8. " *Whoso privily slandereth his neighbour, him will I cut off: him that hath an high look and a proud heart will not I suffer. Mine eyes shall be upon the faithful of the land, that they may dwell with me: he that walketh in a perfect way, he shall serve me. He*

*that worketh deceit shall not dwell within my house : he
that telleth lies shall not tarry in my sight.   I will early
destroy all the wicked of the land ; that I may cut off all
wicked doers from the city of the Lord.*"

Truth and uprightness shall adorn their attendants.
The faithful and the holy shall have office in their house.
Wickedness shall be utterly expelled.   Surely here is a
picture of the blessed household of the King of kings.
It is written, Thy people shall be all righteous : they
shall inherit the land for ever, the branch of My plant-
ing, the work of My hands, that I may be glorified.
If earthly rulers should be surrounded by a godly
retinue, surely this rule will order the celestial court.
Have we by faith put on the garment of salvation, the
spotless robe of Christ's obedience ?   Have we received
the Spirit to sanctify each movement of our hearts ?
Such is the glorious company of the celestial home.

XXXI.

PSALM CII. I–I2.

THE soul trembling under God's displeasure is in extremest anguish. Its misery pours out multitudinous
complaints. Various images lend their aid. Hope is
found only in God and His unchanging love.

———————

1, 2. "*Hear my prayer, O Lord, and let my cry come
unto Thee. Hide not Thy face from me in the day when
I am in trouble; incline Thine ear unto me: in the day
when I call answer me speedily.*"

An inviting hand is always beckoning us to the
mercy-seat. Its gates are widely open. Tender compassion calls us. Abundant promises insure success.
We may draw near boldly and plead the all-atoning
blood. Especially in times of distress are we encouraged to utter the desires of our hearts. We may use
holy violence, and wrestle with our God. We may refuse to give Him rest until responses come. It is not
presumption to be urgent for immediate answers, and
to pray that God would speedily cause His smile to
dissipate our trouble.

3, 4, 5. " *For my days are consumed like smoke, and my
bones are burned as an hearth. My heart is smitten, and
withered like grass; so that I forget to eat my bread. By
reason of the voice of my groaning my bones cleave to my
skin.*

Prayer should be more importunate when sorrows press with overwhelming weight. The effects of such distress are soon apparent. The strength of the frame quickly declines. It vanishes like the curling smoke, which rises to evaporate in air. The bones wax feeble, and crumble to decay as fuel on the burning hearth. Mourning withers all energy. The grass when cut soon becomes dry and sapless, so the smitten heart loses all freshness. The appetite declines. There is no desire for food, no relish for the customary sustenance. Misery finds vent in moans and sighs, so that the flesh is wasted, and the form moves as a living skeleton.

6, 7. "*I am like a pelican of the wilderness : I am like an owl of the desert. I watch, and am as a sparrow alone upon the house-top.*"

Images from nature aid the portrait of this misery. The afflicted shuns all companionship. He retires as the lonely pelican, seeking the solitude of the wilderness, or, as the owl, hiding in the recesses of the desert. Alone he utters wails to heaven, as a solitary sparrow moping on the summits of the house.

8, 9, 10, 11. "*Mine enemies reproach me all the day ; and they that are mad against me are sworn against me. For I have eaten ashes like bread, and mingled my drink with weeping, because of Thine indignation and Thy wrath : for Thou hast lifted me up, and cast me down. My days are like a shadow that declineth ; and I am withered like grass.*"

Misery is enhanced by the cruel mockery of the ungodly. No compassion melts their hearts. They rather joy to aggravate the sufferer's woe. No comfort is found in natural refreshment. Bread is rejected, as unpalatable ashes, and tears are mingled with the cup. Again we hear that the days are as a fleeting shadow, and as the withered grass. The cause of this misery is the withdrawal of God's presence. The mercies once so dear are hidden in displeasure.

12. *" But Thou, O Lord, shalt endure for ever, and Thy remembrance unto all generations."*

But let the fear never intrude that there is variableness with God. He is unchangeable in all His attributes. There may be change in outward manifestations, but He ever lives the One eternal and immutable. Let this thought be cherished constantly. Let it be as a companion ever walking by our side. Let our delighted gaze dwell on the eternal oneness of our God. His power and love endure for ever. All generations shall give this testimony.

XXXII

PSALM CII. 13–28.

13, 14. "*Thou shalt arise, and have mercy upon Zion: for the time to favour her, yea, the set time, is come. For Thy servants take pleasure in her stones, and favour the dust thereof.*"

Apparently the scene now changes. A sorrowing individual disappears. An afflicted people becomes prominent. It is a sound conclusion, that the Psalmist was thus inspired, when signs announced Israel's near deliverance from distress. Her children had long wept under oppression's heavy hand: but now the set time of sorrow reached its close, and the set time of deliverance dawned. It is a blessed truth, that God works all things after the counsel of His own will. When He decrees the rescue, the tyrant's hand can no more fetter. Ardent longings had arisen that the temple should again be built. God Who has power to move all hearts now awakened this desire. We know, too, that Israel's sons shall be recalled from their long dispersion. When we see growing anxiety to hasten their return, we trust that this awakening is heaven-born, and indicates that the set time is drawing near.

15, 16. "*So the heathen shall fear the name of the Lord, and all the kings of the earth Thy glory. When the Lord shall build up Zion, He shall appear in His glory.*"

The return of Israel, the rebuilding of Jerusalem, the rising again of God's temple were grand events; and attracted world-wide attention. It was seen that the

Lord's power was put forth to accomplish restoration. Heathen nations acknowledged God's hand, and viewed with awe His majesty. So again when Israel's glory is revived, it shall be admiration through the world.

17, 18, 19, 20, 21, 22. *" He will regard the prayer of the destitute, and not despise their prayer. This shall be written for the generation to come : and the people which shall be created shall praise the Lord. For He hath looked down from the height of His sanctuary ; from heaven did the Lord behold the earth. To hear the groaning of the prisoner ; to loose those that are appointed to death. To declare the name of the Lord in Zion, and His praise in Jerusalem. When the people are gathered together, and the kingdoms, to serve the Lord."*

At the appointed time, redoubled cries for aid were heard. Mercy spread rapid wings. Again the time draws near when the groanings of the dispersed shall wax more deep. Heaven will open wide to help, and God's praises shall again resound throughout Jerusalem.

23, 24. *" He weakened my strength in the way ; He shortened my days. I said, O my God, take me not away in the midst of my days : Thy years are throughout all generations."*

This deliverance is wholly the Lord's work. Man's innate strength is as cradled infancy. The feeble pilgrim totters if not upheld. Appeal is made unto God. His never-failing power pervades all time. To trust in self is to lean on emptiness. To trust in the Lord is sure support. As He was in the beginning, so will He be for evermore.

25, 26, 27, 28. *" Of old hast Thou laid the foundation of the earth ; and the heavens are the work of Thy hands.*

They shall perish, but Thou shalt endure ; yea, all of them shall wax old like a garment : as a vesture shalt Thou change them, and they shall be changed. But Thou art the same, and Thy years shall have no end. The children of Thy servants shall continue, and their seed shall be established before Thee."

Bright and glorious is this conclusion. The Spirit teaches that this splendid picture exhibits the blessed Jesus. In the beginning the heavens and the earth were His work. When the consummation is complete, the scaffold shall be taken down, and this frame-work shall be laid aside as a decayed vest. But to Him no age shall come. Throughout eternity His redeemed shall praise Him and magnify His glorious name. Let us now learn the happy art. Let us go forth in lowly contemplation of dissolving nature, and hasten the day when Jesus shall appear arrayed in never-ending glory, and admired in all them that believe.

XXXIII.

PSALM CIII.

As in the firmament one star differeth from another
star in glory, so this hymn shines with surpassing lustre.
Through a long course of years it has been especial
comfort to the Church. May it be especial comfort to
our hearts!

1, 2. *" Bless the Lord, O my soul ; and all that is within me, bless His holy name. Bless the Lord, O my soul,
and forget not all His benefits."*
Praise is a plant of heavenly growth. It is the
saint's choice garden of delights. Drowsy souls should
be stirred up, and every faculty quickened to expend
its language. Heaven is opened wide to pour down
benefits. Every benefit should be received with adoration. Abundant crops of praise should spring from this
abundant seed.
3, 4, 5. *" Who forgiveth all thine iniquities; who
healeth all thy diseases. Who redeemeth thy life from destruction ; who crowneth thee with loving-kindness and
tender mercies. Who satisfieth thy mouth with good
things ; so that thy youth is renewed like the eagle's."*
A throng of mercies crowd upon our view. Each
presents large themes of praise. Who can bless God
enough that He is ever ready to pardon—that He has

provided a fountain in His dear Son's blood to wash out
every iniquity. It is a soul-transporting truth that they
who hide in the Saviour's wounds are screened for ever
from His wrath. But the believer, though heir of forgiveness, is ever prone to fall into unhealthy malady.
It is a true description, The whole head is sick—
and the whole heart faint—from the sole of the foot to
the crown of the head there is nothing in us but
wounds and bruises and putrifying sores. Can these
diseases be all healed ?   Jesus is full remedy.   He
gives health and a cure. He is Jehovah-Rophi.   To
Him, too, we may bring every malady of our sickly
frames.   During His earthly ministry diseases fled
before Him.   As many as touched Him were made
perfectly whole. What an encouragement to bring all
sickness unto Him ! He is Jesus still. Who can give
thanks enough for redemption's wonders ! It rescues
us from destruction's grasp. It cries, Deliver him from
going down to the pit : I have found a ransom. Loving-
kindness, too, and tender mercies exalt the believer
to grand eminence. A crown is set upon his head,
sparkling with glory. Rich supplies too of sustenance
are abundantly provided. All things needful to cheer
and to invigorate enrich his board. Thus, though at
times he may appear to droop, he revives, as an eagle,
rising from its languishing to the freshness and vigour
of its youth.

6, 7. " *The Lord executeth righteousness and judgment
for all that are oppressed.   He made known His ways
unto Moses, His acts unto the children of Israel.*"

He especially befriends His children, when oppressed
by cruel foes. He stretches forth His hand to vindi-

cate their cause. In His dealings with Moses and the children of Israel, He draws a chart in which His watchful guidance may be ever traced.

8, 9, 10. " *The Lord is merciful and gracious, slow to anger, and plenteous in mercy. He will not always chide; neither will He keep His anger for ever. He hath not dealt with us after our sins, nor rewarded us according to our iniquities.*"

The Lord's tender dealings are here portrayed. It is Scripture's frequent testimony that He is rich in mercy, and that His mercy endureth for ever. Mercy looks upon our misery and flies to give alleviation. Grace, too, is its close comrade. It compassionates demerits. It brings the robe of Christ's righteousness to cover our unworthiness. We are quick to sin. But our God is long-suffering. He pauses and restrains due vengeance. The plenitude of His goodness outweighs the plenitude of our guilt. When He chides it is His strange work. The scourge is soon checked, and smiles of love dispel the frowns of wrath. Who can regard our mountains of mountains of iniquity, and not confess, We are undone. If God should dispense strict justice to our sins, we perish. But in Christ Jesus free grace triumphs.

XXXIV.

PSALM CIII. 11–22.

11, 12. "*For as the heaven is high above the earth, so great is His mercy toward them that fear Him. As far as the east is from the west, so far hath He removed our transgressions from us.*"

Infinitude is borrowed to exemplify God's mercy. Immeasurable distance parts the heaven from earth, so God's mercy exceeds all bounds. Thought cannot conceive it. Words cannot express it. Ransomed souls are its main recipients. They are aptly described as filled with the reverential grace of fear. Infinite space again expresses the removal of our sins. No traversing steps can join the east to west. As we advance from the one the other constantly recedes. Let us bless the Holy Spirit for employing this image to teach how utterly the guilt of sin is cancelled.

13, 14. "*Like as a father pitieth his children, so the Lord pitieth them that fear Him. For He knoweth our frame; He remembereth that we are dust.*"

Sweet is the picture of paternal love. Compassion melts a father's breast. He speaks and acts in constant tenderness. But what is earthly feeling compared to the benevolence of a heavenly Father's heart! He knows, too, our every infirmity. By fellow-feeling Jesus sympathizes with weak humanity.

15, 16, 17, 18. "*As for man, his days are as grass; as a flower of the field, so he flourisheth: for the wind passeth over it, and it is gone; and the place thereof shall know*" *it no more.   But the mercy of the Lord is from everlasting to everlasting upon them that fear Him, and His righteousness unto children's children ; to such as keep His covenant, and to those that remember His commandments to do them."*

This picture shows the frailty and instability of man. Enduring strength is not his property.   Behold the grass of the meadow !   The Word cries, " All flesh is grass." For a little moment it is green and vigorous.   But in a speck of time it is dried up and withered.   Behold, too, the flower of the field !   It presents a lovely form.   But evanescent is its beauty !   A biting wind arises.   Its bright hues all fade.   It disappears and leaves no trace. Its place is vacant. We may search, but it is gone.   View now in contrast the mercy of our God !   It is from everlasting to everlasting.   It endures for ever.   No age can change its loveliness, or dim its beauteous smiles.   So, too, His righteousness beams from generation to generation.   Covenant love blesses His faithful people, whose delight is to be steadfast in His ways, and in whose thoughts His commandments have perpetual sway.

19. *" The Lord hath prepared His throne in the heavens ; and His kingdom ruleth over all."*

Faith is invigorated by contemplating the sovereignty of God.   In heaven He sits as King.   His rule is unbounded over all the inhabitants of earth.   What thought can be more cheering !   What truth can give more solid support !   How safe are they who shelter beneath His wings.   They are kept as the very apple of His eye.   Who can harm them ?   His sheep shall never perish, for who can pluck them out of His hands ?

20, 21, 22. *" Bless the Lord, ye His angels, that excel*

*in strength, that do His commanaments, hearkening unto
the voice of His word.   Bless ye the Lord, all ye His hosts:
ye ministers of His, that do His pleasure.   Bless the Lord,
all His works, in all places of His dominion: bless the
Lord, O my soul."*

Let universal praise pervade all heaven and earth.
Let all the angelic hosts, whose life is uninterrupted
service, shout aloud.   Marvellous powers are their
inheritance.   Let all be consecrated to one work.   Theirs
is the joy of hearkening to His voice.   Let theirs be the
joy of rendering blessing.   Let all creation swell the
strain.   Throughout His realm let silence be unknown.
O my soul, let noblest rapture emanate from thee.   Let
loudest notes attest thy love.

XXXV.

PSALM CIV. 1–18.

A SPLENDID picture is here exhibited of the greatness of God in creation and providence. Vows follow that the praises which are due shall be devoutly rendered.

1. *" Bless the Lord, O my soul. O Lord my God, Thou art very great ; Thou art clothed with honour and majesty."*

A noble opening is herald to this hymn. Let us awaken our souls to render blessings unto Him whose blessing rests on all His works. Is He not worthy ? Truly His greatness is unsearchable. What thought can estimate the honour and majesty which clothe Him !

2, 3. *" Who coverest Thyself with light as with a garment ; who stretchest out the heavens like a curtain ; who layeth the beams of His chambers in the waters ; who maketh the clouds His chariot ; who walketh upon the wings of the wind."*

What mortal eye can look upon His glory ! His robe is light. The sun in all its splendour pales in His presence. When He uplifts the light of His countenance the darkness of sin and ignorance and impurity flee away. Who can proclaim the habitation of His glory ! The heavens enwrap it as a curtain. His chambers rest upon the waters above the firmament. When He comes forth as a mighty potentate, the rolling clouds are represented as His car of state. The mighty

winds expand their wings to be His seat. Let the
image be pondered. Enlargement only weakens.

4. " *Who maketh His angels spirits ; His ministers a
flaming fire.*"

Angels are intelligences created by His will. They are
marvellously formed as spirits without outward frame.
Swiftly do they fly to execute His purpose; brightly do
they shine as kindled flames. Let us give thanks that
they are all created to do His pleasure, and to minister
to them who shall be heirs of salvation.

5, 6, 7, 8, 9. " *Who laid the foundations of the earth,
that it should not be removed for ever. Thou coveredst it
with the deep as with a garment : the waters stood above
the mountains. At Thy rebuke they fled ; at the voice of
Thy thunder they hasted away. They go up by the
mountains ; they go down by the valleys unto the place
which Thou hast founded for them. Thou hast set a
bound that they may not pass over ; that they turn not
again to cover the earth.*"

Behold the earth, which is the work of His hands !
He makes it to rest on solid foundations. No power
can change its form or bring it to decay. Behold, too,
the sea ! It is His, and He made it. Imagination is
encouraged to go forth and view all the waters at His
command rushing into the basin prepared for them, and
forming ocean's wide expanse. View, too, the bound-
aries by which it is encircled. His mighty voice curbs
the wild billows, and says, " Thus far and no further."

10, 11, 12, 13, 14, 15, 16, 17, 18. " *He sendeth the
springs into the valleys, which run among the hills. They
give drink to every beast of the field : the wild asses quench
their thirst. By them shall the fowls of the heaven have*

their habitation, which sing among the branches. He watereth the hills from His chambers: the earth is satisfied with the fruit of Thy works. He causeth the grass to grow for the cattle, and herb for the service of man: that He may bring forth food out of the earth; and wine that maketh glad the heart of man, and oil to make his face to shine, and bread which strengtheneth man's heart. The trees of the Lord are full of sap; the cedars of Lebanon, which He hath planted; where the birds make their nests: as for the stork, the fir-trees are her house. The high hills are a refuge for the wild goats, and the rocks for the conies."

Marvellous is the adaptation of all things to man's comfort. All who breathe the breath of life are objects of God's care. Do they thirst? Springs of water give refreshing supply. Do they hunger? The earth is a board of sufficient food. Creatures untamed by man have also full provision. Branches are supplied on which the songsters of the air give melody. Pre-eminently man's comfort is the main care. There is provision made that his strength should be recruited, and that joy and gladness should sparkle on his brow. The Psalm commenced with, " Bless the Lord," and let us here pause, reiterating, " Bless the Lord, O my soul !"

XXXVI.

PSALM CIV. 19-35

19, 20, 21, 22. "*He appointed the moon for seasons;
the sun knoweth his going down. Thou makest darkness,
and it is night; wherein all the beasts of the forest do creep
forth. The young lions roar after their prey, and seek
their meat from God. The sun ariseth, they gather themselves together, and lay them down in their dens.*"

The devout mind finds rich repast in reading
nature's volume. The construction and maintenance
of the world is a large field for thought to traverse. The
firmament claims foremost admiration. In it two grand
luminaries shine. The sun and moon rule the hours
of work and rest. They know their appointed times.
They move with regularity, ordering the division of
day and night. The light restores recruited powers to
toil. Darkness calls the wild beasts to their prey. The
inmates of the forest are thus heaven's care. They rove
in darkness, and in light seek rest.

23, 24. "*Man goeth forth unto his work, and to his
labour, until the evening. O Lord, how manifold are Thy
works! in wisdom hast Thou made them all: the earth is
full of Thy riches.*"

Man is pre-eminent in heaven's plans. Creation's
order subserves his wants and comforts. Who can ponder
the arrangement without adoring the wisdom of God.
High thought ordains nature's revolving course.

25, 26, 27, 28, 29, 30. "*So is this great and wide sea
wherein are things creeping innumerable, both small and*

great beasts. There go the ships; there is that leviathan, whom Thou hast made to play therein. These wait all upon Thee, that Thou mayest give them their meat in due season. That Thou givest them they gather: Thou openest Thine hand, they are filled with good. Thou hidest Thy face, they are troubled: Thou takest away their breath, they die, and return to their dust. Thou sendest forth Thy Spirit, they are created; and Thou renewest the face of the earth."

Not less marvellous are the provisions of the sea. On its bosom ships ride, transporting men and commerce from clime to clime. Within its depths innumerable creatures roam. Some boast gigantic form; others show the tiniest mould. All receive being from God. He wills, they live. He wills, they disappear. During their brief career all their nourishment is His bounteous gift. Abundance is the offspring of His power. In His open hand all support finds birth. Life and the means of living result from His sovereign will.

31, 32. *" The glory of the Lord shall endure for ever: the Lord shall rejoice in His works. He looketh on the earth, and it trembleth; He toucheth the hills, and they smoke."*

These works have a loud voice proclaiming His glory, which shall last for ever. But in addition to His love and tender care, they moreover prove that His power can frown terribly. At His bidding the trembling earth strikes the inhabitants with awe. The roar and flames of the volcano show that destructions move at His command.

33, 34, 35. *" I will sing unto the Lord as long as I live; I will sing praise to my God while I have my being. My*

*meditation of Him shall be sweet: I will be glad in the
Lord.   Let the sinners be consumed out of the earth, and
let the wicked be no more.   Bless thou the Lord, O my soul.
Praise ye the Lord."*

Heaven-kindled piety sums up the whole.   The devout soul resolves that sweet meditation shall be its
employ, and that joy in the Lord's work shall captivate
the inner man.   It looks onward to the time when sin
shall no more mar the beauties of creation.   Enraptured with the thought, it again stirs up the soul to
sing, and bless, and praise.   But many view with un-
concern these all-instructive scenes.   The loveliness
enchants not.   The skill produces no amaze.   They are
as little moved as if they saw some random-work or
freaks of undirected change.   Alas! what streams of
joy flow by them untasted by their lips.   They hear
not all nature's chorus hymning the Creator's praise.
To them the new heavens and the new earth would
bring no charms.   Whence comes this blinded state?
They know not God.   To know Him is to love His
Word, His will, and all the wonders of His hand.

XXXVII.

PSALM CV. 1–22.

AN earnest call invites to universal praise. The story of God's dealings with His ancient people is used to quicken this hymn.

———

1, 2, 3, 4. *"O give thanks unto the Lord; call upon His name: make known His deeds among the people. Sing unto Him, sing psalms unto Him: talk ye of all His wondrous works. Glory ye in His holy name: let the heart of them rejoice that seek the Lord. Seek the Lord, and His strength; seek His face evermore."*

It is a blessed task to seek the Lord rejoicingly in praise. Supplications should be intermixed. Prayer should awaken praise, and praise enliven prayer. God's mighty deeds afford large scope. It should be incessant joy to recall His wonders, and to encircle them with out-bursts of adoring hymns. Thus let us seek the Lord, and magnify His strength, and come into His presence.

5, 6, 7. *"Remember His marvellous works that He hath done; His wonders, and the judgments of His mouth; O ye seed of Abraham His servant, ye children of Jacob His chosen. He is the Lord our God; His judgments are in all the earth."*

Memory is a precious gift. It places past events in vivid light. Let our minds be as a well-written narra-tive of Israel's story. The especial call here is to the

lineal seed of Abraham. But if we be Christ's, then
are we Abraham's seed, and heirs according to the promise. In His dealings with the fathers of the Church
we may trace our interest in His care.

8, 9, 10, 11, 12. "*He hath remembered His covenant
for ever, the word which He commanded to a thousand
generations : which covenant He made with Abraham, and
His oath unto Isaac ; and confirmed the same unto Jacob
for a law, and to Israel for an everlasting covenant ; saying, Unto thee will I give the land of Canaan, the lot of
your inheritance ; when they were but a few men in number ; yea, very few, and strangers in it.*"

In the plenitude of His grace He called Abraham
from the land of idolatry to be the progenitor of a
mighty nation. He blessed him with rich and large
promises, and He solemnly confirmed the same to the
son in whom his seed was called. He decreed that His
covenant should endure from age to age. He especially
declared that a lovely portion of this earth should be
their abode. Free grace alone was the moving motive
of this favour. At that time Abraham's household was
but a little band, small and homeless. In the promised
Canaan we may behold our heavenly rest. Let faith
clasp the assurance that in due time this rest shall be
our everlasting portion.

13, 14, 15. "*When they went from one nation to
another, from one kingdom to another people, He suffered
no man to do them wrong ; yea, He reproved kings for
their sakes ; saying, Touch not Mine anointed, and do
My prophets no harm.*"

The early story shows them strangers and pilgrims
upon earth. They wandered from place to place. They

were regarded with jealousy by the potentates of this world. Constant perils threatened their destruction. But God was their shield. He suffered no violence to injure.

16, 17, 18, 19, 20, 21, 22. "*Moreover, He called for a famine upon the land; He brake the whole staff of bread. He sent a man before them, even Joseph, who was sold for a servant; whose feet they hurt with fetters: he was laid in iron: until the time that His word came; the word of the Lord tried him. The king sent and loosed him; even the ruler of the people, and let him go free. He made him lord of his house, and ruler of all his substance; to bind his princes at his pleasure, and teach his senators wisdom.*"

They were cradled and nurtured in perilous providences. Famine oppressed them. A favourite son was carried as a slave to Egypt. He was immured in prison and shackled in galling chains. But he emerged to sit beside the monarch on his throne, and to guide the rulers with wise counsels. At every point in this story let us pause and marvel; but at no pause let praise be silent. For love to His chosen is pre-eminently shown. The sun at times might be obscured; but soon the rays resumed their power. Let, then, the truth delight our hearts, I have loved thee with an everlasting love: therefore with loving-kindness have I drawn thee.

XXXVIII.

PSALM CV. 23—45.

23, 24. "Israel also came into Egypt; and Jacob so-journed in the land of Ham. And He increased His people greatly, and made them stronger than their enemies."

Constraining circumstances brought Jacob and his household into Egypt. Here God's smile crowned them with prosperity. Their numbers rapidly increased. The surrounding natives witnessed their growing power. Jealousy was quick to see where strength resided.

25. "He turned their heart to hate His people, to deal subtilly with His servants."

God suffered the vile passions to intensify. The king's heart was hardened and his eyes were blinded. He saw not the all-directing hand of God. Crafty schemes were devised to extirpate. Impiety strove by subtle arts to keep them low.

26. "He sent Moses His servant, and Aaron whom He had chosen."

When God has a purpose to accomplish He raises suitable instruments. His work can never fail because means are insufficient. Is it not written, that of the very stones He can raise up children unto Abraham! So He called Moses and Aaron to their destined posts. They came forth fearless of the tyrant, and exhibited credentials that they were sent of heaven.

27, 28, 29, 30, 31, 32, 33, 34, 35, 36. "They showed His signs among them, and wonders in the land of Ham. He sent darkness, and made it dark; and they rebelled

*not against His word.   He turned their waters into blood,
and slew their fish.   Their land brought forth frogs in
abundance in the chambers of their kings.   He spake, and
there came divers sorts of flies, and lice in all their coasts.
He gave them hail for rain, and flaming fire in their land.
He smote their vines also and their fig-trees, and brake the
trees of their coasts.   He spake, and the locusts came, and
caterpillars, and that without number, and did eat up all
the herbs in their land, and devoured the fruit of their
ground.   He smote also all the first-born in their land,
the chief of all their strength."*

Terrible plagues afflicted the persecuting land.   With
appalling prodigies God showed His wrath.   The sun
concealed its light.   Darkness spread its thickest pall
around.   The trembling people sat in more than midnight gloom.   The waters of their noble river flowed
in blood and poison.   All nature warred against them,
and enwrapped them in hopeless ruin.   Noisome reptiles
filled their houses with distress.   There was no escape.
Herbage withered.   The fruits of the field were blasted.
Death entered into every dwelling, and loud cries be-
wailed the smitten first-born.   God, who never wants
means to save, now sent forth instruments to destroy.

37, 38. *" He brought them forth also with silver and
gold ; and there was not one feeble person among their
tribes.   Egypt was glad when they departed ; for the fear
of them fell upon them."*

His chosen left their bondage enriched with treasures
and invigorated with health.   Egypt, which had exulted
in oppression, was more delighted to witness their
departure.

39, 40, 41, 42, 43, 44, 45. *" He spread a cloud for a*

*covering, and fire to give light in the night.   The people
asked, and He brought quails, and satisfied them with the
bread of heaven.   He opened the rock, and the waters
gushed out ; they ran in the dry places like a river.   For
He remembered His holy promise, and Abraham His
servant.   And He brought forth His people with joy,
and His chosen with gladness ; and gave them the lands
of the heathen ; and they inherited the labour of the people ;
that they might observe His statutes, and keep His laws.
Praise ye the Lord."*

It is sweet profit to contemplate God's gracious care
of Israel in the wilderness, and the power with which
He planted them triumphant in the promised land.
There can be no bounds to the praise thus swelling in
the heart.   By day a cloudy covering was their screen :
by night it brightened into a vast luminary.   At their
request fowls fell in abundance round the camp.   Water
from the smitten rock flowed in their rear.   Not one
word of promise failed.   Goodness and mercy followed
their advancing steps, until they reaped the plenty of
their promised home.   Hallelujah.   Praise ye the Lord.

XXXIX.

PSALM CVI. 1–22.

PRAISE opens and concludes this instructive Psalm. The context is dark in frightful displays of the rebellion and ingratitude of God's people. Bright manifestations of sparing and forgiving grace finally appear.

1, 2. "*Praise ye the Lord. O give thanks unto the Lord; for He is good: for His mercy endureth for ever. Who can utter the mighty acts of the Lord? who can show forth all His praise?*"

By precept and by example we should strive to awaken songs of thanksgiving. A glorious theme animates our minds. Goodness and mercy invite attention. This goodness is unsearchable. This mercy swells as an ocean without shore. Vain, then, are our utmost efforts to uplift adequate strains. If we possessed all the powers of all the angelic hosts, and all the tongues of all whoever breathed, and if they were expanded in one perpetual utterance, they could not measure the due expanse. But the more we strive the more we shall succeed.

3. "*Blessed are they that keep judgment, and he that doeth righteousness at all times.*"

There is no blessedness apart from walking in the fear of God. Let our feet ever traverse this righteous path.

4, 5. "*Remember me, O Lord, with the favour that Thou bearest unto Thy people: O visit me with Thy salvation; that I may see the good of Thy chosen, that I may rejoice in the gladness of Thy nation, that I may glory with Thine inheritance.*"

This aspiration is offspring of heaven. Let us ever look to God to raise us to this height of blessedness. The terms exhort us to fix our delighted gaze on the happiness of God's chosen. Salvation is their property. They realize the pledged enjoyment. But still the blessedness and glory of this inheritance exceed all thought. God, who gave the heirs of salvation to His dear Son, and who gave His Son for them, will with Him also freely give them all things. They are the true inheritors of earth. They soon shall be the inmates of celestial homes, and eternity will not exhaust their bliss.

6, 7. "*We have sinned with our fathers, we have committed iniquity, we have done wickedly. Our fathers understood not Thy wonders in Egypt; they remembered not the multitude of Thy mercies; but provoked Him at the sea, even at the Red Sea.*"

This salvation springs from grace. No merit wins it. We are poor sinners, even as our fathers were. Look back to the deliverance from Egypt. All the tokens of love and tender compassion destroyed not the seeds of iniquity in the favoured nation. Marvellously brought through the Red Sea, they showed proofs that evil still rankled in their hearts.

8, 9, 10, 11. "*Nevertheless He saved them for His name's sake, that He might make His mighty power to be known. He rebuked the Red Sea also, and it was dried up: so He led them through the depths, as through the wilderness.*"

And He saved them from the hand of him that hated them, and redeemed them from the hand of the enemy. And the waters covered their enemies; there was not one of them left."

Long-suffering still endured. Mercy held back the arm of vengeance. Succour and deliverance still magnified His glorious name. They were led safely through the depths of the sea. They were rescued from the cruelty of their enemies, while the returning waters overwhelmed the foes. Every child of Israel was saved; every child of Egypt died.

12, 13, 14, 15. "*Then believed they His words; they sang His praise. They soon forgat His works; they waited not for His counsel; but lusted exceedingly in the wilderness, and tempted God in the desert. And He gave them their request; but sent leanness into their soul.*"

Such loving-kindness for a moment melted them; hymns of praise resounded. But their goodness was like the morning cloud, as the early dew it passed away. In the wilderness they murmured, because their lust for food was not indulged. They impiously tempted God. He granted their desire, but the meat in their mouths was impoverishment in their hearts.

16, 17, 18. "*They envied Moses also in the camp, and Aaron the saint of the Lord. The earth opened and swallowed up Dathan, and covered the company of Abiram. And a fire was kindled in their company; the flame burned up the wicked.*"

They treated their appointed leaders with contempt, and scoffed at their authority. Terrible punishment ensued. The gaping earth swallowed up the rebels. Devouring flames consumed their substance.

19, 20, 21, 22. *" They made a calf in Horeb, and wor-shipped the molten image. Thus they changed their glory into the similitude of an ox that eateth grass. They for-gat God their Saviour, which had done great things in Egypt; wondrous works in the land of Ham, and terrible things by the Red Sea."*

At Horeb they dethroned Jehovah, and exalted as their god the image of a calf. Their hearts relapsed into the idolatry of Egypt. The mighty wonders which marked their deliverance from that tyrannic sway were as a forgotten tale. Let us chide our souls to treasure up the memory of all His benefits.

XL.

PSALM CVI. 23–48.

23. *"Therefore He said that He would destroy them, had not Moses His chosen stood before Him in the breach, to turn away His wrath, lest He should destroy them."*

God's patience had been tried to the extremest point. Just vengeance reared its head.   But Moses interposed. He sought the Lord.   He humbled himself in dust and ashes, and prayed that mercy might still be glorified. The prayer of faith is heard, and longer space is given to the rebellious host.   Let us learn in faith to cry for others.   Such sympathy is welcomed in the courts above. God turned the captivity of Job when he prayed for his friends.

24, 25, 26, 27. *"Yea, they despised the pleasant land; they believed not His word; but murmured in their tents, and hearkened not unto the voice of the Lord.   Therefore He lifted up His hand against them, to overthrow them in the wilderness: to overthrow their seed also among the nations, and to scatter them in the lands."*

Reports were brought of the luxuriant beauty of their future home.   But incredulity derided, and haughty scoffs sneered.   The promise which secured this great inheritance was treated as an empty word.   We see an awful picture of the terrible evil which by nature depraves man's heart.

28, 29, 30, 31. *" They joined themselves also unto Baal-*

peor, and ate the sacrifices of the dead. Thus they pro-
voked Him to anger with their inventions ; and the plague
brake in upon them. Then stood up Phinehas, and exe-
cuted judgment : and so the plague was stayed. And that
was counted unto him for righteousness unto all genera-
tions for evermore."

The filthy pleasures of idolatry. enticed them. They
revelled in guilty scenes of impurity, and feasted on the
idol-offerings. Unblushing iniquity shunned not the
light. Phinehas in holy zeal rushed to vindicate God's
honour. He hastened to deal signal punishment. Thus
he gave evidence that faith was the inmate of his heart.
By this righteous act he obtained acknowledgment that
he was a Spirit-taught believer. Let us be diligent to
give evidence that faith is our living principle.

32, 33. *" They angered Him also at the waters of strife,*
so that it went ill with Moses for their sakes : because they
provoked his spirit, so that he spake unadvisedly with his
lips."

When water failed again their provocation so exceeded that even the meek spirit of Moses was ruffled.
He spake in petulance, and for a moment yielded to
temptation. Sin in God's most faithful servants is sin
still, and calls for tokens of displeasure. Moses suffered
keenly. The decree went forth that his feet should
never tread the longed-for Canaan.

34, 35, 36, 37, 38, 39. *" They did not destroy the na-*
tions, concerning whom the Lord commanded them : but
were mingled among the heathen, and learned their works.
And they served their idols : which were a snare unto them.
Yea, they sacrificed their sons and their daughters unto
devils, and shed innocent blood, even the blood of their sons

*and of their daughters, whom they sacrificed unto the idols
of Canaan: and the land was polluted with blood. Thus
were they defiled with their own works, and went a whor-
ing with their own inventions."*

Surely when they rested in all the comforts of their
desired abode their walk would be undeviating obedience. Surely happiness and love would be the inmates
of their dwellings. Alas! what is man? They spared
the idolaters whom they were commanded to destroy.
They intermingled with their services, and adopted their
abominable vices. They devoted their own children to
accursed devils. The blood of impious sacrifices stained
their hands. No sin appalled them.

40, 41, 42, 43, 44, 45, 46. *" Therefore was the wrath of
the Lord kindled against His people, insomuch that He
abhorred His own inheritance. And He gave them into
the hand of the heathen; and they that hated them ruled
over them. Their enemies also oppressed them, and they
were brought into subjection under their hand. Many
times did He deliver them; but they provoked Him with
their counsel, and were brought low for their iniquity.
Nevertheless He regarded their affliction when He heard
their cry: and He remembered for them His covenant,
and repented according to the multitude of His mercies.
He made them also to be pitied of all those that carried
them captives."*

Signal judgments followed. Invaders subjugated
their land. Oppressed, they cried again, and were delivered only to sin more.

47, 48. *" Save us, O Lord our God, and gather us from
among the heathen, to give thanks unto Thy holy name,
and to triumph in Thy praise. Blessed be the Lord God*

*of Israel from everlasting to everlasting: and let all the
people say, Amen.   Praise ye the Lord."*

The result should stimulate us to be more diligent in
prayer and praise.   Let all within us cry, Save us, good
Lord, and we will bless Thy name.   Dangers are always
near.   Sacred records warn us.   Our experience con-
firms the truth.   It is madness to hope for safety from
our own vigilance or strength.   They fall who trust in
such unstable ground.   Let our eyes be ever on the
Lord, so shall we triumph in His praise.

XLI.

PSALM CVII. 1–22.

EXHORTATION to thanksgiving is the first note of this Psalm. Various motives follow. Man is exhibited in divers straits and difficulties, and God appears in the plenitude of His grace.

1. " *O give thanks unto the Lord, for He is good ; for His mercy endureth for ever.*"

Calls to thanksgiving cannot be too frequently renewed. Overflowing streams of mercy follow the redeemed during all their days. Each instance has a voice loudly crying, Give thanks, give praise. Let our heart-strings be strained to the utmost to uplift adoration.

2, 3. " *Let the redeemed of the Lord say so, whom He hath redeemed from the hand of the enemy ; and gathered them out of the lands, from the east, and from the west, from the north, and from the south.*"

Surely this will be the constant note of all, who realize redemption. They once were in thraldom to the power of darkness, but are rescued by the mighty arm of Jesus. The Saviour has shivered the sceptre of their arch-enemy. He has opened their prison-doors, and has translated them into the kingdom of their God. Loud should be their present song. Soon shall they be gathered safely to their eternal home; and the great

multitude, which no man can number, of all nations
and kindreds, and peoples, and tongues shall upraise
the universal Hallelujah!

4, 5, 6, 7, 8, 9. " *They wandered in the wilderness
in a solitary way; they found no city to dwell in.
Hungry and thirsty, their soul fainted in them. Then
they cried unto the Lord in their trouble, and He delivered them out of their distresses. And He led them
forth by the right way, that they might go to a city of
habitation. Oh that men would praise the Lord for His
goodness, and for His wonderful works to the children
of men! For He satisfieth the longing soul, and filleth
the hungry soul with goodness.*"

This is a graphic description of wanderers and exiles.
In it we see the children of Israel in their tedious
journeyings; but it especially portrays the outcast condition in which the redeemed often mourn. Their souls
are tossed on restless billows. They wander and stray.
They long for repose, but they find it not. They are
exposed to every peril. They require support, and
know not how to obtain it. At last they turn to God,
and direct their cries to Him. He speedily arises, and
their difficulties vanish. Oh that the saints would feel
that He is guiding them aright, and that soon their end
will be welcome admission to the heaven of heavens!
A new chorus follows: Oh that men would praise the
Lord for His goodness, and for His wonderful works to
the children of men. All desires are satisfied. Goodness meets all cravings. God's wonder-working hand
has strewed blessings around.

10, 11, 12, 13, 14, 15, 16. " *Such as sit in darkness, and in the shadow of death, being bound in affliction*

*and iron ; because they rebelled against the words of God,
and contemned the counsel of the most High : Therefore
He brought down their heart with labour : they fell
down, and there was none to help. Then they cried unto
the Lord in their trouble, and He saved them out of their
distresses. He brought them out of darkness and the
shadow of death, and brake their bands in sunder. Oh
that men would praise the Lord for His goodness, and
for His wonderful works to the children of men ! For
He hath broken the gates of brass, and cut the bars of
iron in sunder."*

Forgetful of all God's goodness, His people are prone
to scorn His counsels, and to rebel against His gracious
authority. The sure consequence is due chastisement.
The rejection of His easy yoke leads to the darkness of
the prison-house, and to the shackles of the iron chains.
But still there is hope. God lives, mighty to deliver;
to Him they cry, and deliverance comes on speedy
wings. Let the chorus sound again: Oh that men
would praise the Lord for His goodness, and for His
wonderful works to the children of men. His people
rejoice in liberty; the prison-gates are burst asunder;
the bars of iron are shivered.

17, 18, 19, 20, 21, 22. *"Fools, because of their
transgression, and because of their iniquities, are afflicted :
their soul abhorreth all manner of meat ; and they draw
near unto the gates of death. Then they cry unto the
Lord in their trouble, and He saveth them out of their
distresses. He sent His word, and healed them, and
delivered them from their destructions. Oh that men
would praise the Lord for His goodness, and for His
wonderful works to the children of men ! And let them*

sacrifice the sacrifices of thanksgiving, and declare His works with rejoicing."

Senseless men will rush into transgression. Divers afflictions follow. The wasted body rejects all nourishment. At last prayer revives, and prayer is a prevailing power. God's word, which commanded sickness, commands the return of health. Again the chorus sounds—again thanksgivings multiply: Oh that men would praise the Lord for His goodness, and for His wonderful works to the children of men. And let them sacrifice the sacrifices of thanksgiving, and declare His works with rejoicing. Let His altar be laden with utterances of adoring love. Thus let merited misery vanish in incense of pious joy.

XLII.

PSALM CVII. 23–42.

23, 24, 25, 26, 27. "*They that go down to the sea in ships, that do business in great waters; these see the works of the Lord, and His wonders in the deep. For He commandeth, and raiseth the stormy wind, which lifteth up the waves thereof. They mount up to the heaven, they go down again to the depths; their soul is melted because of trouble. They reel to and fro, and stagger like a drunken man, and are at their wit's end.*"

One of nature's most astounding scenes here meets us. The sea is lashed into terrific fury. The staggering mariners are bewildered. Whence arises this terror? What is the cause of this dismay? The Lord sent forth His voice. The obedient billows reflect His will. They raise gigantic heads; they threaten to invade the highest heights of heaven. Again they descend, as if to search the lowest depths, and to penetrate into its deepest caverns. The affrighted mariners no longer can retain firm step. They tremble with the trembling ship, and no resources give relief.

28, 29, 30, 31, 32. "*Then they cry unto the Lord in their trouble, and He bringeth them out of their distresses. He maketh the storm a calm, so that the waves thereof are still. Then are they glad because they be quiet; so He bringeth them unto their desired haven. Oh that men would praise the Lord for His goodness, and for His wonderful works to the children of men! Let them exalt*

*Him also in the congregation of the people, and praise
Him in the assembly of the elders."*

God sits above the tempest's rage. To Him in their
affright the shipmen cry. He never turns from prayer.
He hears, and lulls the storm. Behold His mighty
power! His will softens the raging lion into the gentle
lamb. We are reminded of our Jesus in the storm on
the Sea of Galilee. He rebuked the winds and waves,
and perfect calm ensued. The rejoicing mariners see
God's wondrous hand, and reach in safety the haven
which they sought. A sea of perils often threatens to
engulf believers. But let them pray and trust. Their
souls need fear no shipwreck. The glad chorus again
sounds rapturously: Oh that men would praise the
Lord for His goodness, and for His wonderful works to
the children of men! Let them exalt Him also in the
congregation of the people, and praise Him in the
assembly of elders. Let them praise Him in the secret
of their chambers; let them praise Him when His
assembled people celebrate holy worship.

33, 34, 35, 36, 37, 38, 39, 40, 41. *" He turneth rivers
into a wilderness, and the water-springs into dry ground;
a fruitful land into barrenness, for the wickedness of them
that dwell therein. He turneth the wilderness into a
standing water, and dry ground into water-springs. And
there He maketh the hungry to dwell, that they may pre-
pare a city for habitation; and sow the fields, and plant
vineyards, which may yield fruits of increase. He blesseth
them also, so that they are multiplied greatly, and suffereth
not their cattle to decrease. Again, they are minished,
and brought low through oppression, affliction, and sorrow.
He poureth contempt upon princes, and causeth them to*

*wander in the wilderness, where there is no way.   Yet
setteth He the poor on high from affliction, and maketh
Him families like a flock."*

The earth sees vicissitudes of fertility and dearth.
The waters of the rivers cease.   The verdant fields become a barren waste.   Again the wilderness is fertilized
by springs.   The fields receive the seed.   The grapes
hang in clusters.   The mightiest princes are brought
low.   The poor and needy are crowned with plenty.
These wonders are wrought by God's hand.   All things
obey His word.   They are recorded for our admonition.

42, 43. *" The righteous shall see it, and rejoice ; and
all iniquity shall stop her mouth.   Whoso is wise, and
will observe these things, even they shall understand the
loving-kindness of the Lord."*

God's people ponder these wondrous works.   With joy
and gladness they recognize His hand ; while the wicked
must hang down their heads in silence.   Let God's
dealings be our constant study.   They give marvellous
instruction.   The crowning lesson is, that God is
loving, faithful, true.

XLIII.

PSALM CVIII.

THE Psalmist professes immovable resolve to make praise his incessant joy. He prays for support against all opponents, and avows his confidence in full reply.

———

1, 2. "*O God, my heart is fixed; I will sing and give praise, even with my glory. Awake, psaltery and harp; I myself will awake early.*"

By nature the heart is fickle, roving, inconstant. What it seeks to-day, it shuns to-morrow. But grace brings a blessed change. All the affections are then firmly fixed on God. We love Him because He has first loved us. Love in the heart cannot but be praise on the lips. The tongue, which is man's glory, as his distinction from the brute creation, will be consecrated to Him. It is our glory when it gives glory to the Lord. Not the tongue only, but all means within our reach will be pressed into this service. From the earliest dawn praise will be heard. Returning consciousness shall resume the work.

3, 4. "*I will praise Thee, O Lord, among the people: and I will sing praises unto Thee among the nations. For Thy mercy is great above the heavens, and Thy truth reacheth unto the clouds.*"

Praise will not be limited to the retirement of the closet. It will sound aloud when pious congregations meet. From the lips of missionaries it will traverse distant lands. The theme is ever grand. Never can it weary. It tells of mercy which is higher than the heights above, and of truth which is as unassailable as the pinnacles of heaven.

5, 6. "*Be Thou exalted, O God, above the heavens; and Thy glory above all the earth; that Thy beloved may be delivered: save with Thy right hand, and answer me.*"

No efforts can sufficiently exalt our God. When we have striven to our utmost power we have scarcely reached the borders of our theme. Let prayer, too, be intermingled. We should supplicate deliverance from every foe, and answers to our every cry.

7, 8, 9, 10. "*God hath spoken in His holiness; I will rejoice, I will divide Shechem, and mete out the valley of Succoth. Gilead is mine; Manasseh is mine; Ephraim also is the strength of mine head; Judah is my lawgiver; Moab is my wash-pot; over Edom will I cast out my shoe; over Philistia will I triumph. Who will bring me into the strong city? who will lead me into Edom?*"

Faith remembers that a holy God has dealt out holy promises. These give abundance of unwavering assurance. The Psalmist looks around and sees what conquests he has obtained over surrounding cities and peoples. Thus he fears not though strong cities may yet remain in open defiance. He will reign in triumph over mightiest potentates.

11, 12, 13. "*Wilt not Thou, O God, who hast cast us off? and wilt not Thou, O God, go forth with our hosts? Give us help from trouble: for vain is the help of man. Through God we shall do valiantly: for He it is that shall tread down our enemies.*"

No fears should weaken. Faith is assured that God, who has given help, will help to the end. For a little time the enemy may seem to succeed. Brief is the appearance. Final victory is sure. But let there be no trust in an arm of flesh. Human policy and resolves are slender props. Man in his best estate is the shadow of a shade. But if God upholds, strong and valiant will be the arm, and triumphs will be near. Shall we not praise, and pray, and trust, knowing that the Lord of hosts is with us, and that omnipotence is our sword ? Let faith go forth and behold the servants of the Lord doing valiant exploits in the Christian warfare, and marching over the necks of their enemies to the triumphant throne of glory.

XLIV.

PSALM CIX.

A TERRIBLE train of miseries awaits the enemies of our heavenly King. As each sorrow passes in review may we draw nearer to our blessed Lord, in whom alone there is shelter and peace.

1, 2, 3, 4, 5. *" Hold not Thy peace, O God of my praise; for the mouth of the wicked, and the mouth of the deceitful, are opened against me: they have spoken against me with a lying tongue. They compassed me about also with words of hatred; and fought against me without a cause. For my love they are my adversaries; but I give myself unto prayer. And they have rewarded me evil for good, and hatred for my love."*

We cannot doubt that the sufferings of Jesus are conspicuous in this psalm. The Holy Spirit distinctly exhibits Judas as the antitype of this awful description. We should regard it, moreover, as prophetic of the doom of all who raise the voice, and contrive plots against the gracious Saviour. He appeals unto His heavenly Father. He calls Him to mark the iniquity which encompassed Him. He complained of the cruel requital which His tender love experienced. He meekly adds, that while hatred was their life, His life was un-interrupted prayer. May every trial drive us to the mercy-seat!

6, 7, 8, 9, 10, 11, 12, 13, 14, 15, 16, 17, 18, 19, 20.
" *Set Thou a wicked man over him; and let Satan stand
at his right hand. When he shall be judged, let him be
condemned; and let his prayer become sin. Let his days
be few; and let another take his office. Let his children
be fatherless, and his wife a widow. Let his children be
continually vagabonds, and beg: let them seek their bread
also out of their desolate places. Let the extortioner catch
all that he hath; and let the strangers spoil his labour.
Let there be none to extend mercy unto him; neither let
there be any to favour his fatherless children. Let his
posterity be cut off; and in the generation following let
their name be blotted out. Let the iniquity of his fathers
be remembered with the Lord; and let not the sin of his
mother be blotted out. Let them be before the Lord continually, that He may cut off the memory of them from
the earth. Because that he remembered not to show mercy,
but persecuted the poor and needy man, that he might even
slay the broken in heart. As he loved cursing, so let it
come unto him; as he delighted not in blessing, so let it
be far from him. As he clothed himself with cursing
like as with his garment, so let it come into his bowels like
water, and like oil into his bones. Let it be unto him as
the garment which covereth him, and for a girdle wherewith he is girded continually. Let this be the reward of
mine adversaries from the Lord, and of them that speak
evil against my soul.*"

It is fearful to contemplate these enumerated miseries!
They terribly exhibit what sin deserves, and what just
vengeance will inflict. Can we bless God enough if we
have been rescued from such awful doom, and if the
heart of enmity has been taken from us, and the heart

of love and praise bestowed? Such mercy is the gift
of free and sovereign grace. Let us adore and praise.

21, 22, 23, 24, 25, 26, 27, 28, 29. *"But do thou for
me, O God the Lord, for Thy name's sake: because Thy
mercy is good, deliver Thou me. For I am poor and
needy, and my heart is wounded within me. I am gone
like the shadow when it declineth: I am tossed up and
down as the locust. My knees are weak through fasting;
and my flesh faileth of fatness. I became also a reproach
unto them: when they looked upon me they shaked their
heads. Help me, O Lord my God: O save me according
to Thy mercy; that they may know that this is Thy hand;
that Thou, Lord, hast done it. Let them curse, but bless
Thou: when they arise, let them be ashamed; but let Thy
servant rejoice. Let mine adversaries be clothed with
shame; and let them cover themselves with their own confusion, as with a mantle."*

The believer is deeply conscious of his weakness,
misery, and need. All His strength resides in God.
Unto God, therefore, incessant prayer should speed.
Saving grace puts forth its energy, and shows violent
agony at the mercy-seat.

30, 31. *"I will greatly praise the Lord with my mouth;
yea, I will praise Him among the multitude. For He
shall stand at the right hand of the poor, to save him from
those that condemn his soul."*

It is sweet relief to close this appalling psalm with
the melody of thanksgiving. The presence of God is
proclaimed as the heritage of His children. He ever
stands at their right hand to deliver them from every
foe. Blessed are the children of the blessed and ever
blessing God.

XLV.

PSALM CX.

A MAGNIFICENT display of the exaltation and sovereignty
of Christ as High Priest of the Church is exhibited.   It
is delight to study this glorious office.   The contemplation tends to sanctify.   May it mould us into heavenly
likeness !

———————

1. " *The Lord said unto my Lord, Sit Thou at my right
hand, until I make Thine enemies Thy footstool.*"

Let us give thanks for every revelation of Christ.
We can only see Him as the Father by the Spirit shall
withdraw the veil.   But here we are invited to contemplate His glorious session at the right hand of all pre-
eminence.   There He wields the sceptre of universal
supremacy.   In mad rebellion many foes defy ; but
they must lie prostrate at His feet.   The word is everlasting truth, Those mine enemies that would not that
I should reign over them bring hither and slay them
before Me.   When His chariot-wheels of triumph shall
crush the enemies, may we shout loyally, Lo ! this is
our God ; we have waited for Him ; He will save us !

2. " *The Lord shall send the rod of Thy strength out
of Zion : rule Thou in the midst of Thine enemies.*"

The all-conquering instrument of this triumph is the
proclamation of His truth from Zion, the type of His
Church.   This word when applied by the Spirit rides

gloriously. No sophistry of man can gainsay. The
rock is softened, and the heart of enmity melts into
love. Thus in the midst of enemies the omnipotence
of His kingdom rules. May this weapon beat down
every hostile feeling of rebellious nature. Let our constant desire be, 'Come in Thou to whom we vow allegiance. Take to Thyself Thy great power, and reign
within us as ruler of every thought.

3. *" Thy people shall be willing in the day of Thy
power, in the beauties of holiness from the womb of the
morning : Thou hast the dew of Thy youth."*
The Lord well knows His own. " Thine they were,
and Thou gavest them Me." When He utters His
attractive call they flock to Him on delighted wings.
They swiftly fly as doves to their windows. Shining
in the beauties of holiness, He attracts and captivates.
His converts are innumerable, as the morning dew-
drops of the lawn. They shall be multiplied as the
sparkling gems which descend at dawn from heaven.

4. *" The Lord hath sworn, and will not repent, Thou
art a priest for ever after the order of Melchizedek."*
Endless glories adorn our blessed Lord. As He is
our King, so, too, He is our Priest. The Father's oath
invests Him as successor of Melchizedek. As our
Priest He brings Himself the all-atoning victim to the
altar of the cross. As our Priest He enters the Holy
of Holies, and sprinkles the expiating blood. As our
Priest He bears our names upon His heart. As our
Priest He blesses us with all the blessings which heaven
can bestow. Jesu, we adore Thee as our High Priest
for ever.

5, 6, 7. *" The Lord at Thy right hand shall strike*

through kings in the day of His wrath. He shall judge among the heathen, He shall fill the places with the dead bodies; He shall wound the heads over many countries. He shall drink of the brook in the way: therefore shall He lift up the head."

All the powers of heaven encircle His banner. Throughout the world His triumphs shall be known. They who have raised the rebel-arm shall be ground to powder. In His all-glorious work sustaining refreshment shall cheer Him. For the joy that was set before Him He endured the cross, despising the shame, and is set down at the right hand of the throne of God. What brook can more invigorate the thirsty traveller. Streams of reviving joy are flowing by our side. The invitation has gone forth, Drink, yea drink abundantly, O beloved.

XLVI.

PSALM CXI.

PRAISE is the one theme of this enrapturing Psalm. Various motives call to this homage. May they all excite response in our adoring hearts!

---

1. "*Praise ye the Lord. I will praise the Lord with my whole heart, in the assembly of the upright, and in the congregation.*"

Praise is the tribute which never can be fully paid. Beginning in time, it will swell throughout eternity. Not only should our lips joy in this grace; we should exhort others to the godly exercise. Precept should enforce the duty; example should mark out the path. This praise should issue from hearts overflowing with grateful love. Shame on all meagre utterance and all cold expression! The whole heart, with every affection, should be rapturously engaged. We should thus testify our love, not only in seasons of retirement, but publicly in the assemblies of the sanctuary.

2, 3, 4. "*The works of the Lord are great, sought out of all them that have pleasure therein. His work is honourable and glorious; and His righteousness endureth for ever. He hath made His wonderful works to be remembered: the Lord is gracious, and full of compassion.*"

Calls to praise exceed all number. The works of His hands ever supply matter. They are a treasure-

house of wonders. They are worthy of our constant
study. The more we discover, the more we shall find
fulness of delight. As our pleasure expands, the more
praise should blaze as a flaming torch. His works, too,
are all worthy of Himself. They reflect the glory of
His righteousness. This feature is indelibly stamped
on all. As time rolls on these works endure. The
remembrance of them has immortal life. From generation to generation they declare His essence, and testify
that grace and tenderness ever flow from His throne.

5, 6. "*He hath given meat unto them that fear Him:
He will ever be mindful of His covenant. He hath
showed His people the power of His works, that He may
give them the heritage of the heathen.*"

Ample provision satisfies the wants of His people.
Tender care watches over them. In all this marvellous arrangement, these gracious dealings proclaim
Him as our faithful Father. The everlasting covenant
in Christ secures unfailing blessings. This covenant
never can be broken. Hence the stream of blessings
never can be stayed. Special wonders were exhibited
to His chosen people of old. The heathen were driven
out, that they might occupy the promised inheritance.

7, 8. "*The works of His hands are verity and judgment: all His commandments are sure. They stand
fast for ever and ever, and are done in truth and uprightness.*"

The works of the Lord are echoes to the glories of
His word. They are the accomplishment of His sure
promises. They are bright mirrors in which we may
read His verity and judgment. No power of opposing
foes can contravene His decrees. While we read His

truth in all the wonders of His hand, let us abound
more in grateful thanksgiving.

9, 10. " *He sent redemption unto His people ; He hath
commanded His covenant for ever : holy and reverend
is His name. The fear of the Lord is the beginning of
wisdom : a good understanding have all they that do
His commandments : His praise endureth for ever.*"

The bright crown of His works is the redemption of
His people. This is the substance of His everlasting
covenant. It is our wisdom to regard with awe the
marvels of His dealings. Let us fear and love. Let
us love and praise.

XLVII.

PSALM CXII.

AN exhortation to praise is the herald of this Psalm.
The blessedness of God's children is then set forth.
May its bright colours reveal more of the happiness of
those who by the faith of Jesus compose this family!

---

1. "*Praise ye the Lord. Blessed is the man that
feareth the Lord, that delighteth greatly in His commandments.*"

Let it be our hearts' constant effort to revel in thanksgivings. The matter can never be exhausted. It is
the seed of a luxuriant crop. Let its measure be com-
mensurate. Let us praise God that He is the Father
of a blessed family. The main lineaments are the
same in every child. Filial fear is the common feature.
They love their Father, and they tremble lest they
should offend. They love their Father, and therefore
they delight greatly in obedience to His word.

2, 3. "*His seed shall be mighty upon earth: the generation of the upright shall be blessed. Wealth and riches
shall be in his house; and his righteousness endureth for
ever.*"

The godly seed truly inherit the earth. It may be
that gold and silver may not sparkle in their homes;
but they are endowed with the treasures of peace and
joy, compared with which earthly possessions are an
empty show. The world may scorn them, but they are

kings and priests unto God. Godliness is true greatness, which rust and moth destroy not, and spoilers
cannot touch.

4, 5. " *Unto the upright there ariseth light in the darkness: He is gracious, and full of compassion, and righteous. A good man showeth favour, and lendeth: he will
guide his affairs with discretion.*"

The heirs of heaven are not exempt from days of
gloom. Shadows come over them, and bright rays fade.
Such discipline is often needed. It checks the erring
steps. It draws to God's presence. It quickens faith
and prayer. But transient are these seasons. Light
soon breaks forth, and God's love brightly re-appears.
Every grace, too, is the inmate of the believer's heart.
Especially he regards tenderly the need of others, and
is ever ready, as his means enable, to extend aid. His
heart, too, is the abode of the truest wisdom. They are
the fools who neither seek nor serve the Lord. This
wisdom is conspicuous in every transaction. He who
serves God will not err in his daily matters.

6, 7, 8. " *Surely he shall not be moved for ever: the
righteous shall be in everlasting remembrance. He shall
not be afraid of evil tidings: his heart is fixed, trusting in
the Lord. His heart is established, he shall not be afraid,
until he see his desire upon his enemies.*"

He stands immovable as a rock. His confidence is
firmly settled on his God. He trembles not lest messengers should announce calamities. He knows that
all events are ordered by his heavenly Father, and
therefore that all things must work together for his
good. He fears not lest his foes should gain advantage,
and extinguish his remembrance upon earth.

9, 10. "*He hath dispersed, he hath given to the poor; his righteousness endureth for ever; his horn shall be exalted with honour.　The wicked shall see it, and be grieved; he shall gnash with his teeth, and melt away: the desire of the wicked shall perish.*"

While the righteous are thus blessed and exalted and glorified, there is a fearful counterpart.　The ungodly see the issue.　They writhe in anguish.　Lord, give us our portion in the happy family of faith!

XLVIII.

PSALM CXIII.

PRAISE continues to be the happy theme. Contemplation of God's majesty and greatness and goodness tend
largely to kindle this flame. Let us meditate until
warmth glows and praise blazes within!

1, 2. " *Praise ye the Lord. Praise, O ye servants of the
Lord, praise the name of the Lord. Blessed be the name
of the Lord from this time forth and for evermore.*"

The servants of the Lord are addressed. They are
called to their richest enjoyment. They who serve the
Lord prove how they love His service by ever telling the
glories of His name. It is the constellation of His
attributes, and each attribute presents a boundless
ocean of delight. Praise, too, must be endless. Through
endless being they who know and love Him will
never cease to revel in this joy. Praise is as eternal as
the love which kindles it.

3. " *From the rising of the sun, unto the going down
of the same, the Lord's name is to be praised.*"

Is there a spot on earth which is not witness of God's
goodness? Is there a region of the globe in which this
homage should not abound? Is there a living being
who is not partaker of His tender mercies? Is there a
mother's son who should not testify thanksgiving?

From east to west, from pole to pole, the constant sound should be adoring praise.

4, 5, 6. " *The Lord is high above all nations, and His glory above the heavens. Who is like unto the Lord our God, who dwelleth on high, who humbleth Himself to behold the things that are in heaven, and in the earth !*"

What is all the pride, and pomp, and pageantry of earth ! All nations and all nations' greatness is a mere bauble when placed beside Him. What property is there which is not the gift of His sovereign hand? Behold His throne. It is high in the heaven of heavens. From it He looks down in condescension on angels and on men. The more we wonder that He thus should stoop, the more we should exalt Him with extolling lips.

7, 8, 9. " *He raiseth up the poor out of the dust, and lifteth the needy out of the dunghill; that He may set him with princes, even with the princes of his people. He maketh the barren woman to keep house, and to be a joyful mother of children. Praise ye the Lord.*"

God's gracious eye regards even the lowliest of men with providential care. Joseph rises from the dungeon to sit beside the King. David is exalted from the sheepfold to the throne of Israel. Sarah rejoices as the mother of him in whom the promised seed should come. Rachel and Hannah are filled with maternal joy. There is nothing too hard for our Lord to do. No gift is too good for His bounty to impart. "Praise ye the Lord" was the first note. "Praise ye the Lord" is now the last. "Praise ye the Lord" should be our utterance first, midst, and last in time and throughout eternity.

XLIX.

PSALM CXIV.

THE greatness and the glory of God are shown in His dealings with Israel. Let us joyfully remember that this God is our God for ever and ever.

———————

1, 2. "*When Israel went out of Egypt, the house of Jacob from a people of strange language; Judah was His sanctuary, and Israel His dominion.*"

Grievous was Israel's thraldom in the land of Egypt. They were oppressed by tyrants, aliens in blood and speech. Their history should remind us that when we were lost by sin God sent redemption through His beloved Son, and called us into the kingdom of liberty and grace. Israel thus delivered was raised to be a peculiar people. They were consecrated to the service of the Lord. They had His sanctuary and His laws, His temple and His ordinances. The priestly office solemnized its rites, and God was acknowledged as their King. So, too, we are no more our own. We are ransomed, that we may delight in His ordinances and serve Him as our rightful Lord.

3, 4. "*The sea saw it, and fled; Jordan was driven back. The mountains skipped like rams, and the little hills like lambs.*"

When the set time of deliverance is come, no obstacles can check. The waters of the Red Sea seem to forbid escape from Egypt. The waters of Jordan seem to forbid entrance into Canaan. But at God's word they parted, and there was a dry passage for the hosts. Thus departure from perils was effected; thus entrance into the promised land was gained. Let faith take courage. The same power still works. The chosen seed shall depart in triumph from the captivity of Satan, and in triumph enter their eternal home. In Israel's march, too, astounding prodigies were shown. The strongest mountains trembled at God's presence and the gaping earth obeyed His mandates. Mighty powers are arrayed in opposition to God's people; but when the Lord speaks, trembling and quaking shake their might. "Who art thou, O great mountain; before Zerubbabel, thou shalt become a plain."

5, 6, 7, 8. " *What ailed thee, O thou sea, that thou fleddest? thou Jordan, that thou wast driven back? Ye mountains, that ye skipped like rams; and ye little hills, like lambs? Tremble, thou earth, at the presence of the Lord, at the presence of the God of Jacob; which turned the rock into a standing water, the flint into a fountain of waters.*"

These marvellous interpositions were the direct acts of God. No natural causes produced these prodigies. This truth is enforced by lively questions addressed to inanimate objects. The presence of the Lord effected all. We next are reminded that providential care supplied their wants in the wilderness: the flinty rock melted, ..nd streams in abundance flowed. These emblems teach that God's people shall have every want relieved. "When the poor and needy seek water, and there is none, and their tongue faileth for thirst, I the Lord will hear them; I the God of Jacob will not forsake them." O Lord, be it unto us according to Thy gracious word! Supply all our need, according to Thy riches in glory by Christ Jesus!

L.

PSALM CXV.

MAN's utter nothingness is here acknowledged. In God alone all power resides. The idols of the heathen are the vanity of vanities. Let all confidence be placed in God!

---

1. "*Not unto us, O Lord, not unto us, but unto Thy name give glory, for Thy mercy, and for Thy truth's sake.*"

Piety shudders at the thought of the assumption of any power by man. We cannot sink too low. We cannot raise our God too high. There is no depth from which we may not look up to Him. Let the assurance be always ours that His mercy and His truth will certainly befriend.

2, 3. "*Wherefore should the heathen say, Where is now their God? But our God is in the heavens: He hath done whatsoever He hath pleased.*"

Israel was often brought into heathen bondage. Insulting foes derided them as helpless, and tauntingly inquired, Where is their God? The reply was indisputable. God reigns on high. Heaven is His throne. His overruling hand moves everywhere. He works all things after the counsel of His own will.

4, 5, 6, 7, 8. "*Their idols are silver and gold, the work of men's hands. They have mouths, but they speak not; eyes have they, but they see not; they have ears, but they*

*hear not ; noses have they, but they smell not ; they have
hands, but they handle not ; feet have they, but they walk
not ; neither speak they through their throat. They that
make them are like unto them ; so is every one that trusteth
in them."*

What can be more contemptible than the idols of the
heathen world ! These images may be cased in silver
and in gold. They may shine dazzlingly in the sight
of prostrate crowds. But emptiness is their only property. Blind, deaf, motionless, speechless, they are less
than nothing. Their worshippers are scarcely better.
Where are the minds of those who kneel before the
workmanship of their own hands ! But while we pity
such degraded folly, let us never forget that creature-
worship is nature's religion. The love of silver and
gold is innate idolatry of heart.

9, 10, 11. *" O Israel, trust thou in the Lord : He is their
help and their shield. O house of Aaron, trust in the
Lord ; He is their help and their shield. Ye that fear
the Lord, trust in the Lord : He is their help and their
shield."*

From a view of worthless idols, the exhortation gains
force to trust in the ever-living God, who has all power
in heaven and in earth. Let all His people trust Him.
Let all who fear Him trust Him. Especially let the
ministers of His word be foremost in this holy confidence. The standard-bearers should precede the host.
They have all cause to trust. He is ever ready and
ever able to give help. His sure protection can never
fail.

12, 13, 14, 15. *" The Lord hath been mindful of us :
He will bless us ; He will bless the house of Israel ; He*

will bless the house of Aaron : He will bless them that
fear the Lord, both small and great.   The Lord shall in-
crease you more and more, you and your children.   Ye are
blessed of the Lord, which made heaven and earth."

The review of the past testifies of the ever-mindful
hand of God.   Each Ebenezer gives assurance that
blessings will still incessantly descend.   Though ap-
pearances may sometimes have an adverse look, yet
from age to age generations of men shall rejoice under
His gracious care.   He hath delivered us, and still delivers, and we trust that He will yet deliver us.

16, 17, 18. " *The heaven, even the heavens, are the*
Lord's ; but the earth hath He given to the children of
men.   The dead praise not the Lord, neither any that go
down into silence.   But we will bless the Lord from this
time forth and for evermore.   Praise the Lord."

While we continue inhabitants of earth our lips may
praise the Lord, and uplift adorations to the heavens.
But our life here may be very brief.   Our opportunities
may quickly pass.   Lips mute in the grave can no
more be heard on earth.   Let us bear in mind, too, that
dead souls on earth cannot have spiritual employ.   Let
us then pray, Quicken us, good Lord, more and more.
The tribute of praise shall then respond in louder and
holier notes.

LI.

PSALM CXVI.

THE heart of the Psalmist overflows with gratitude for signal mercies. They all demand devoted praise. May the effect on us be increase of heavenly-mindedness!

1, 2. "*I love the Lord, because He hath heard my voice and my supplications. Because He hath inclined His ear unto me, therefore will I call upon Him as long as I live.*"

Senseless is he who ever disregards the answer to the voice of prayer. These answers sweetly constrain us to love the gracious Lord, whose ears are never closed. Moreover, we are thus encouraged to wax more diligent in supplicating cries. The more we pray, the more we gain. The more we gain, the more should we love and adore.

3, 4. "*The sorrows of death compassed me, and the pains of hell gat hold upon me: I found trouble and sorrow. Then called I upon the name of the Lord; O Lord, I beseech thee deliver my soul.*"

Believers are ofttimes brought into the lowest depths of distress. Life seems as a flickering spark; but in all extremities prayer can seek aid and never seeks in vain.

5, 6. "*Gracious is the Lord and righteous; yea, our God is merciful. The Lord preserveth the simple: I was brought low, and He helped me.*"

The God to whom we thus draw near is full of grace. Tender compassion is ever warm within Him. Experience of this truth is the believer's firmest prop. In frequent need he has never found that help to fail.

7, 8, 9. "*Return unto thy rest, O my soul; for the Lord hath dealt bountifully with thee. For Thou hast delivered my soul from death, mine eyes from tears, and my feet from falling. I will walk before the Lord in the land of the living.*"

Troubles may tend to bring disquietude; but the knowledge of near deliverance keeps peace undisturbed. Under Christ's shadow the soul delights in sweet repose. "Thou wilt keep him in perfect peace whose mind is stayed on Thee." Can he be tossed with fears and doubts who rests in Christ as his ark? Where is the fear of death? It has vanished. A gracious hand, too, wipes away all tears from the eye: the feet, too, no longer totter, but walk firmly in the way of life.

10, 11, 12, 13, 14. "*I believed, therefore have I spoken: I was greatly afflicted. I said in my haste, All men are liars. What shall I render unto the Lord for all His benefits toward me? I will take the cup of salvation, and call upon the name of the Lord. I will pay my vows unto the Lord now in the presence of all His people.*"

Faith is no silent grace. When it is lively in the heart the mouth will celebrate God's praise. Severity of affliction awakens its powers. It is not slow to confess that when it slumbered, hastiness and unseemly utterances found vent. In disregard of all assurances, pettishness prevailed ; but the Psalmist in dark hours had thought that fulfilment would not come. But now he felt shame for such distrust. He remembers the holy rites, he vows that he will gladly drink the cup of blessing, and publicly redeem his promises of holy service.

15. *" Precious in the sight of the Lord is the death of His saints."*

Persecution may wildly rage against God's servants. Their lives may be regarded as mere chaff ; but different is God's estimate ! They are precious in His sight : and the high value placed upon them will be evidenced by the signal retribution which will overtake the cruel murderers.

16, 17, 18, 19. *"O Lord, truly I am Thy servant ; I am Thy servant, and the son of Thine handmaid : Thou hast loosed my bonds. I will offer to Thee the sacrifice of thanksgiving, and will call upon the name of the Lord. I will pay my vows unto the Lord now in the presence of all His people, in the courts of the Lord's house, in the midst of thee, O Jerusalem. Praise ye the Lord."*

Happy is the profession, O Lord, truly I am Thy servant ! Consecration to God's service is perfect freedom. It is the very happiness of happiness, and raises to angelic life. But to abound in this employ, Satan's chains must be broken. This only can be effected by the might of Jesus. We are born slaves. He only can set us free. This devotion, too, is a theme of praise and of holy vows. Let us surrender ourselves to this one work. We shall find that we obey a blessed Master, who will pay wages now of abundant happiness and of eternal life hereafter.

LII.

PSALM CXVII.

THIS Psalm is brief, but who can estimate its unbounded preciousness.   It was given by inspiration
of God.   May the Spirit use it to invigorate our grace!

1. *"O praise the Lord, all ye nations: praise Him,
all ye people."*

Warm desire should swell in every heart that due
praise to God should be as the surrounding atmosphere.
Throughout the world no creature lives who is not daily
laden with blessings from the Creator's hand.   Sad it
is that the blinded eye sees not the gracious Giver, and
the dumb lips give no acknowledgment.   This thought
should quicken missionary zeal.   Warm should be our
efforts to send the messengers of truth throughout the
length and breadth of earth.   The constant desire should
be to tell of God's love in Jesus, and to invite to the
cross.   Hearty praise will then sound loudly from ransomed souls.

2. *"For His merciful kindness is great toward us:
and the truth of the Lord endureth for ever.   Praise ye
the Lord."*

The merciful kindness of the Lord is a boundless
theme.   We see it inscribed on all the works of creation.
We see it shining in the glories of redemption.   What
could have been done more for His people that the Lord

hath not done for us ? The great God, even Jesus, is our full salvation. There is pardon in His precious blood for every sin. There is a covering robe in His righteousness for every transgression. There is sanctification and renewal in His Spirit for our cold hearts. The cup of grace, of mercy, and of love verily overflows. It could scarcely hold another drop. The promises of the covenant are all yea and amen in Christ. Could God give more ? Let, then, our grateful cry ever swell, Praise ye the Lord.

LIII.

PSALM CXVIII.

A SONG of praise is here added to our stores. Motives
to this exercise claim attention. In many portions
Christ is distinctly seen. May He thus become dearer
to our hearts!

———————

1, 2, 3, 4. " *O give thanks unto the Lord; for He is
good: because His mercy endureth for ever. Let Israel
now say, that His mercy endureth for ever. Let the house
of Aaron now say, that His mercy endureth for ever. Let
them now that fear the Lord say, that His mercy endureth
for ever.*"

Our sluggish hearts cannot be too thankful for
exhortations to sing of mercy. All classes, all ranks
should be incessantly earnest in this duty. Let God's
ministering servants lead the hymn. Let all the
company of believers respond, " His mercy endureth
for ever."

5, 6, 7. " *I called upon the Lord in distress: the Lord
answered me, and set me in a large place. The Lord is
on my side; I will not fear: what can man do unto
me? The Lord taketh my part with them that help
me; therefore shall I see my desire upon them that
hate me.*"

Faith hears Christ in these professions. He speaks
not in His own person only, but as representing all His

people. Let us, then, cast away all fear. God in Him
and He in us is triumph over every foe.

8, 9, 10, 11, 12. "*It is better to trust in the Lord than
to put confidence in man: it is better to trust in the Lord
than to put confidence in princes. All nations compassed
me about: but in the name of the Lord will I destroy
them. They compassed me about; yea, they compassed me
about: but in the name of the Lord I will destroy them.
They compassed me about like bees: they are quenched as
the fire of thorns: for in the name of the Lord I will
destroy them.*"

To trust in the Lord is help and victory. To trust in
man is to walk on a quicksand. May the Lord raise
us above such folly! Our great Head here testifies for
Himself and for His followers, that though His enemies
might be countless in number and terrible in sting, they
must vanish before the presence of the Lord.

13, 14, 15, 16. "*Thou hast thrust sore at me, that I
might fall: but the Lord helped me. The Lord is my
strength and song, and is become my salvation. The voice
of rejoicing and salvation is in the tabernacles of the
righteous: the right hand of the Lord doeth valiantly.
The right hand of the Lord is exalted: the right hand of
the Lord doeth valiantly.*"

We should be grateful for these precious assurances.
Mighty, indeed, is our main adversary, but he is as
nothing before the Lord. In our God we have all
strength and all salvation. His right hand will fight
mightily and triumphantly in our behalf. Thus the
voice of thanksgiving shall be heard in our homes.

17, 18, 19, 20, 21. "*I shall not die, but live, and declare the works of the Lord. The Lord hath chastened me*

*sore : but He hath not given me over unto death.   Open to
me the gates of righteousness : I will go into them, and I
will praise the Lord : this gate of the Lord, into which the
righteous shall enter.   I will praise Thee : for Thou hast
heard me, and art become my salvation.*"

We are again warned that, though our feet stand on
the rock of salvation, we are not beyond the reach of
trials.   But let nothing shake our confidence.   The
praises of the Lord shall yet be our song.

22, 23, 24. "*The stone which the builders refused is
become the head stone of the corner.   This is the Lord's
doing : it is marvellous in our eyes.   This is the day
which the Lord hath made ; we will rejoice and be glad
in it.*"

Christ is again manifest.   He has been, and He still
is, the despised and rejected of men.   But He is the
foundation on which His Church rests, and the orna-
ment of the beauteous fabric.   It was a glorious day
when, rising from the dead, He was displayed as the
Son of God.   It is indeed to each believer a glorious
day when He shines in their hearts as all their salvation.

25, 26, 27, 28, 29. "*Save now, I beseech Thee, O Lord :
O Lord, I beseech Thee, send now prosperity.   Blessed be
he that cometh in the name of the Lord : we have blessed
you out of the house of the Lord.   God is the Lord, which
hath showed us light : bind the sacrifice with cords, even
unto the horns of the altar.   Thou art my God, and I will
praise Thee : Thou art my God, I will exalt Thee.   O give
thanks unto the Lord ; for He is good : for His mercy
endureth for ever.*"

Shall we not bless Him who comes in the name of

the Lord ? Shall we not bring our hearts and souls as a willing sacrifice to Him ? While we live let us bless and serve Him. This will be our glad employ throughout eternity. Let the song now begin which never can conclude, " His mercy endureth for ever."

LIV.

PSALM CXIX. 1–8.

1. *"Blessed are the undefiled in the way, who walk in the law of the Lord."*

Here is a glowing picture of the pious heart. Here is the inner life of those who sit on the high eminence of blessedness, and rank among the blessed of the Lord. The question cannot be repressed, Who are they to whom such dignity belongs? The clear reply here meets us, They are the undefiled in the way, they walk in the law of the Lord. It is a solemn truth, that the path of life is through a miry road. Our steps are in pollution's land. How, then, can our feet be undefiled! How can our garments be unsoiled! We cannot guide ourselves. Unaided, we stumble into sloughs of defilement. But all help is near. Jesus is at hand to keep us by His mighty power. Let us lean on His supporting arm at every step, and when we fall let us rise and wash our robes in His all-cleansing blood. So may we ever be among the undefiled in the way; and let the law of the Lord, lovely in purity, glorious in holiness, perfect in love, be the path in which our feet advance. Jesus is our model and our all. God's law was in His heart: He was its living portrait.

2. *"Blessed are they that keep His testimonies, and that seek Him with the whole heart."*

Again, we learn that holiness is blessedness. Let our constant prayer wax stronger, Lord, what wilt Thou have us to do? The reply is, Study the testimonies. They speak from heaven, loud as the thunder, clear as the light, sweet as the celestial songs. Let us thus seek His will, with our whole hearts united in the one pursuit.

3. "*They also do no iniquity: they walk in His ways.*"

The blessed cannot consent to evil. They flee the downward path. They shun it with extreme abhorrence. Their hearts entirely love the heavenward way. They cling to it with undeviating tread. Their onward progress is always upward. Thus they advance in happiness towards heaven.

4. "*Thou hast commanded us to keep Thy precepts diligently.*"

He who desires our good at all times issues with authority His sovereign commands. They enjoin us to adhere with diligence to the tract which His Word marks out. In strict obedience is real and unfailing happiness. To obey is heaven begun.

5. "*Oh that my ways were directed to keep Thy statutes !*"

But when the heart is willing the flesh is weak. Proneness to err still threatens to mislead. Hence incessant desires besiege Heaven that directing grace may ever guide aright.

6. "*Then shall I not be ashamed, when I have respect unto all Thy commandments.*"

Shame and confusion are the wages of them who disregard God's will. If our hearts condemn us, God is greater than our hearts and knoweth all things. If our hearts condemn us not, we shall lift up our heads in joy.

7. " *I will praise Thee with uprightness of heart, when I shall have learned Thy righteous judgments.*"

The blessed man is ever a pupil in God's school. He desires to learn the ways of righteousness. Thus upright praises will ever flow from his lips.

8. " *I will keep Thy statutes: O forsake me not utterly.*"

Firm are his resolves, but he well knows that utter weakness may consist with strong desires. Experience has taught that when we would do good evil is present. He knows that real strength is heaven-born; hence earnest cries implore that God at all times would uphold graciously. He hateth putting away.

LV.

PSALM CXIX. 9–16.

9. *" Wherewithal shall a young man cleanse his way ?
By taking heed thereto according to Thy word."*

Peculiar temptations plot against the young. Passions are strong; experience is weak. Satan assails with unremitted art. But still there is escape. Abundant records speak of holy youths. They have pursued one course. God's Word has been their compass. By this guidance they have diligently steered through all the waves of peril.

10. *" With my whole heart have I sought Thee: O
let me not wander from Thy commandments."*

Sincerity is here avowed. Blessed are they who can thus truly appeal to God. May our conscience ever bear witness that no portion of the heart has been given to ungodly ways! But still God's help is asked, that the way may be so hedged up that no outlet to forbidden paths may be found. We may run well and yet may stumble.

11. *" Thy word have I hid in mine heart, that I
might not sin against Thee."*

It is a precious truth that God's Word is a sure antidote to sin. If this be treasured in the heart, if it stand as a guard before the portals, evil cannot enter May we ever be thus garrisoned !

12. *" Blessed art Thou, O Lord: teach me Thy
statutes."*

The blessed man will ever bless and ever pray.   His constant cry will be, Send out Thy light and Thy truth, that they may lead me!

13. " *With my lips have I declared all the judgments of Thy mouth.*"

He will learn that he may teach. His heart, filled with the Word, will overflow and fertilize all who are within his reach.

14. " *I have rejoiced in the way of Thy testimonies, as much as in all riches.*"

The Word is a bright sunbeam in the soul. Riches do not so much exhilarate the worldling as the revelation of God's ways delight and gladden the blessed man.

15. " *I will meditate in Thy precepts, and have respect unto Thy ways.*"

Holy meditation exalts above the world. The precepts are a perpetual feast.

16. " *I will delight myself in Thy statutes: I will not forget Thy word.*"

Do we seek happiness? It is to be found in constantly pondering the Word and will of God. It is a blessed resolve: Thy Word shall not depart out of the precincts of my memory.

LVI.

PSALM CXIX. 17–24.

17. "*Deal bountifully with Thy servant, that I may live and keep Thy word.*"

We may humbly ask continuance of earthly life, if our desire is that as mirrors we may reflect the Word. Oh that we might live as a transcript of the heavenly will, and thus be followers of God as dear children!

18. "*Open Thou mine eyes, that I may behold wondrous things out of Thy law.*"

Lovely light may beam upon us, and wondrous scenes surround; but the gain is none if sightless eyes survey. By nature we are thus blind: unless God grants sight, we cannot behold the wonders which His law contains. Let us weary heaven with cries for enlightening grace. When the command goes forth, Let there be light, there will be light.

19. "*I am a stranger in the earth; hide not Thy commandments from me.*"

Here we are pilgrims in a foreign land. As such we need guidance. God's Word will show the right path and keep us in it. Let us pray that this word may brightly illumine our way. If we walk in darkness, it is because we see not the light.

20. "*My soul breaketh for the longing that it hath unto Thy judgments at all times.*"

Weak and wavering desires should be utterly eschewed. The true child of God so longs for the precious

Word, that his soul seems scarcely able to contain the swelling feeling. Unless the presence of God's Word relieves, he can scarcely live.

21. "*Thou hast rebuked the proud that are cursed, which do err from Thy commandments.*"

We have heard who are the blessed. We have now the portrait of the cursed. They proudly wander from the everlasting way. Their straying feet rush to destruction. God's rebuke descends, and the rebuke is ruin.

22. "*Remove from me reproach and contempt; for I have kept Thy testimonies.*"

The pious are generally regarded with scorn in this fallen world. It is a grievous trial. When we are conscious that contempt is incurred by adhering to God's Word, we may humbly pray for its removal.

23. "*Princes also did sit and speak against me: but Thy servant did meditate in Thy statutes.*"

Men of exalted rank too often calumniate the servants of the Lord. But a sweet refuge is always near in meditation on the glorious law. They will not hear nor heed whose souls are thus engaged.

24. "*Thy testimonies also are my delight and my counsellors.*"

Such meditation is most precious. It is a boundless expanse of happiness. It is a treasury of counsels to guide throughout life's course. May we be thus happy and thus wise!

LVII.

PSALM CXIX. 25–32.

25. "*My soul cleaveth unto the dust: quicken Thou me according to Thy word.*"

The soul by nature rises not to heaven: unaided from on high it grovels in the mire of earth. Hence the wisdom of constant prayer, that spiritual life may expand wings for upward flight. Many promises give prospect of success.

26. "*I have declared my ways, and Thou heardest me: teach me Thy statutes.*"

Having deep experience of the success of prayer, let us keep nothing back from God. He will hear, and heavenly lessons will be granted.

27. "*Make me to understand the way of Thy precepts: so shall I talk of Thy wondrous works.*"

Our desire for intelligence in God's precepts cannot be too earnest. When thus enlightened we shall not be mute. Delighted converse will tell the dealings of Him whose name is Wonderful.

28. "*My soul melteth for heaviness: strengthen Thou me according unto Thy word.*"

Periods recur when the soul is heavy laden. When thus powerless, strength should be implored in accordance with the sure promises of God.

29. "*Remove from me the way of lying; and grant me Thy law graciously.*"

Grievous evidence of the fall is seen in the tendency

to misrepresent and to deceive. The devil was a liar from the beginning; and his progeny inherits his propensities. Let us strive to be the followers of Him who is emphatically the truth. For this purpose let us pray that God would write His law of uprightness on our hearts.

30. "*I have chosen the way of truth; Thy judgments have I laid before me.*"

False ways will indeed be eschewed by the blessed man. The way of truth will be his deliberate choice. God's judgments will be the desired path. Let us not, however, forget that in ourselves we are weak to execute these good resolves.

31. "*I have stuck unto Thy testimonies: O Lord, put me not to shame.*"

With clinging hands the testimonies will be grasped. The disgrace of straying will be dreaded. Prayer will be made for deliverance from such shame.

32. "*I will run the way of Thy commandments, when Thou shalt enlarge my heart.*"

The narrowness of the contracted heart forbids expanse. Encumbered affections cannot mount; hence earnest prayer is made that the entangling chains may be removed, and freedom granted to run nimbly up the blessed road.

LVIII.

PSALM CXIX. 33-40.

33. " *Teach me, O Lord, the way of Thy statutes, and I shall keep it unto the end.*"

The believer, conscious of ignorance, ever seeks divine instruction. He knows that the page of Scripture is obscure unless heavenly light shines on it. Hence constant is his prayer, and constant his resolve to persevere unto the end.

34. " *Give me understanding, and I shall keep Thy law; yea, I shall observe it with my whole heart.*"

Repeated prayer wrestles for an understanding heart. Resolution is declared that the law shall be cherished with undivided affection.

35. " *Make me to go in the path of Thy command-ments; for therein do I delight.*"

Prayer again wrestles for strict adherence to the holy path. It is the way of pleasantness; every step abounds in delights.

36. " *Incline my heart unto Thy testimonies, and not to covetousness.*"

Without a restraining hand the heart is prone to turn aside into the bye-ways of petty love of pelf. The remedy must be from above. Heavenly aid is therefore sought.

37. " *Turn away mine eyes from beholding vanity; and quicken Thou me in Thy way.*"

The world abounds with sights of emptiness,

frivolity, and folly. Eyes are enticed to gaze; there is danger in the very sight. Let prayer be made that the eyes may not behold, and that quickened steps may ascend Zion's hill.

38. "*Stablish Thy word unto Thy servant, who is devoted to Thy fear.*"

It is happiness to have the Word firmly rooted in the heart. This blessed state will be the desire of those who are jealously apprehensive of straying from the gospel-rule.

39. "*Turn away my reproach which I fear; for Thy judgments are good.*"

It is a reproach to wander. The godly man will dread this shame. He knows how excellent are the ways of God, and he prays that he may never incur the dishonour of disobedience.

40. "*Behold, I have longed after Thy precepts; quicken me in Thy righteousness.*"

Deep desire for entire sanctification is here expressed; prayer is made that the Spirit of the Lord would animate the pursuit of righteousness. May we thus ever strive! We shall succeed, and great will be our gain.

LIX.

PSALM CXIX. 41–48.

41. *" Let Thy mercies come also unto me, O Lord, even Thy salvation, according to Thy word."*

This prayer is a cup filled to the brim. A multitude of tender mercies stand always ready to issue from the courts above. These mercies assure of salvation from the penalties and power of sin, and of welcome to the joys of heaven. These mercies are our promised heritage. How should we wrestle until they fill us to overflowing!

42. *" So shall I have wherewith to answer him that reproacheth me : for I trust in Thy word."*

When the heart realizes assured salvation, it is supplied with abundant answers to those who sneer at the delights of faith.

43. *" And take not the word of truth utterly out of my mouth ; for I have hoped in Thy judgments."*

Assurance only lives while God maintains it. Fears will intrude lest the truth should languish on our lips. Hope sees the declarations of the Lord, and looks upward.

44. *" So shall I keep Thy law continually, for ever and ever."*

There is rich comfort in the confidence that divine grace will enable us to persevere. The end is seen. Bright is the deliverance.

45. *" And I will walk at liberty : for I seek Thy precepts."*

All restraining shackles shall be cast off. The believer will freely walk in diligent pursuit of truth.

46. "*I will speak of Thy testimonies also before kings, and will not be ashamed.*"

No array of earthly power will intimidate the man of God. Strong in the Lord, he will boldly wave the standard of salvation.

47. "*And I will delight myself in Thy commandments, which I have loved.*"

Who can fail to see the believer's happy state! The paths of holiness are pleasantness and peace. The law reigns in the heart, and love delights in sanctified obedience.

48. "*My hands also will I lift up unto Thy commandments, which I have loved; and I will meditate in Thy statutes.*"

He will give open testimony of his entire surrender to the ways of the Lord, and his mind will revel in holy meditation. Here the soul finds repose. This is the ecstasy of life.

LX.

PSALM CXIX. 49–56.

49. "*Remember the word unto Thy servant, upon which Thou hast caused me to hope.*"

The Spirit in tender love sometimes applies a word of Scripture with especial power to the heart. Hope grasps it, feasts upon it, and sweetly reposes. We may in faith bring such texts unto the mercy-seat, and crave their fulfilment. "Do as Thou hast said."

50. "*This is my comfort in my affliction: for Thy word hath quickened me.*"

Many are the afflictions of the righteous; many, too, are their consolations. Especially sweet are the comforts flowing from the Word. Life thus quickened will be sustained.

51. "*The proud have had me greatly in derision; yet have I not declined from Thy law.*"

Haughty men may scorn and deride. Ridicule shakes not the confidence which the Word has inspired. Can man pull down what God has built up?

52. "*I remembered Thy judgments of old, O Lord; and have comforted myself.*"

It is a profitable lesson to ponder God's righteous dealings. The history of the Church is a precious volume. It shows the overthrow of the wicked and constant security of the righteous. Deep streams of comfort flow in these channels.

53. "*Horror hath taken hold upon me because of the wicked that forsake Thy law.*"

M

How frightful is the sight of the ungodly trampling on God's precious Word! Who can contemplate the issue without fearful trembling!

54. "*Thy statutes have been my songs in the house of my pilgrimage.*"

Zion's pilgrims are not always downcast. They realize absence from home; but in the cheering prospect of return they know joy and gladness, thanksgiving and the voice of melody.

55. "*I have remembered Thy name, O Lord, in the night, and have kept Thy law.*"

If in the night sleepless hours are appointed, let memory be alert to ponder the wonders involved in the Lord's name. The resolve will thus be quickened to cling tightly to His law.

56. "*This I had, because I kept Thy precepts.*"

This rich gain springs from keeping His commandments. May they ever be the treasure of our hearts, the path of our steps, and our exceeding comfort!

LXI.

PSALM CXIX. 57-64.

57. " *Thou art my portion, O Lord : I have said that I would keep Thy words.*"

Rich, indeed, is the believer. He has the Lord for his portion. He can say, All things are mine, for I am Christ's, and Christ is God's. The kingdom into which he is translated has statutes. He loves them, and delights to cleave most closely to them.

58. " *I entreated Thy favour with my whole heart : be merciful unto me according to Thy word.*"

With earnest sincerity the heart seeks that heavenly favour may never cease to bless. Mercy is abundantly promised, and mercy may be sought with undoubting confidence that it will smile abundantly.

59. " *I thought on my ways, and turned my feet unto Thy testimonies.*"

No inconsiderate step should ever be allowed; a rash movement may plunge into inextricable straits. The feet should be diligently turned to the narrow way of life. Vigilance should never be relaxed.

60. " *I made haste, and delayed not to keep Thy commandments.*"

Loitering in the Christian course is perilous. Onward, onward should be the constant cry. Lot's wife paused, and then looked back, and perished. Let us lay aside every weight and run unweariedly in the way which love and wisdom have enjoined.

61. " *The bands of the wicked have robbed me: but I have not forgotten Thy law.*"

The godly may be called to bear the spoiling of their temporal goods. But they have riches which no robber's hands can touch. The Word is a treasure in which they daily meditate, with no fear of loss.

62. " *At midnight I will rise to give thanks unto Thee because of Thy righteous judgments.*"

When sleep fast locked the eyes of others, the Psalmist leaves his bed. He is intent to utter praises. God's righteous judgments call for joyful notice. Thanksgiving is repose of the heart.

63. " *I am a companion of all them that fear Thee, and of them that keep Thy precepts.*"

The sincerity of grace is evidenced by the choice of associates. Two cannot walk together except they be agreed. Light has no fellowship with darkness. The feet cannot at the same time be set in the narrow and in the broad way. They who fear God delight in pious fellowship.

64. " *The earth, O Lord, is full of Thy mercy: teach me Thy statutes.*"

The whole creation has a voice loudly proclaiming that good and gracious is the Lord. Every object reflects tender care. Let us seek enlarged knowledge of His works, so will His ways be our delight. Increased illumination will gladden the meditating heart. Advance in knowledge will be advance in joy.

LXII.

PSALM CXIX. 65–72.

65. " *Thou hast dealt well with Thy servant, O Lord, according unto Thy word.*"

Where is the believer who can restrain this rapturous acknowledgment! Touched by divine grace he feels that God's goodness baffles all thought. He knows that our God has given largely like a God. All the provisions of the Covenant are bountifully poured into his lap.

66. " *Teach me good judgment and knowledge : for I have believed Thy commandments.*"

The soul is athirst for brighter rays of light and knowledge. Faith is confessed to be the happy inmate of the heart: and the constant cry is, Give large increase. Faith has sweet skill in pleading.

67. " *Before I was afflicted I went astray ; but now have I kept Thy word.*"

Afflictions are often charged to do good work. Their commission is mercy. A thin disguise conceals a friendly form. They check the wanderers and bring them back. In the time of suffering they may be bitter, but in retrospect they are sweet. They lead to holiness, and holiness is joy.

68. " *Thou art good, and doest good : teach me Thy statutes.*"

The believer delights in contemplation of his God. Every view discovers goodness. This is inscribed on all His dealings. Hence the longing desire for more acquaintance with His statutes. To know His law is to know Himself.

69. *" The proud have forged a lie against me: but I will keep Thy precepts with my whole heart."*

Lying witnesses were suborned to bring false charges against Jesus. If the Head was thus calumniated, shall the members escape? But these arch devices are all vain. They lead to closer adherence to God's Word.

70. *" Their heart is as fat as grease: but I delight in Thy law."*

Their heart swells with pride, and becomes impervious to tender impression. Prosperity often exerts benumbing influence. No sense of sin—no self-abhorrence is its fruit. But there is a lovely contrast. In the believer the contrite heart loathes self-satisfaction, and finds no joy but in clinging to the law of God.

71. *" It is good for me that I have been afflicted: that I might learn Thy statutes."*

Corrupt nature needs the frequent scourge. The present smart may be severe, but the resulting benefit is more than conpensation for the pain. Satisfaction makes rich amends for the sorrows which preceded it. Let not our frowns then meet affliction.

72. *" The law of Thy mouth is better unto me than thousands of gold and silver."*

True is the testimony that the Word of the Lord is more to be desired than gold, yea, than much fine gold. This treasure is in our hands. May the Spirit write its contents on our hearts! God's law inscribed there is everlasting wealth.

LXIII.

PSALM CXIX. 73–80.

73. " *Thy hands have made me, and fashioned me: give me understanding, that I may learn Thy commandments.*"

Appeal is made to God as our Creator. Every faculty of mind and body is the offspring of His sovereign will. Hence He who gives our every power is implored to increase spiritual intelligence. In His school blessed lessons are learned.

74. " *They that fear Thee will be glad when they see me ; because I have hoped in Thy word.*"

Our course should be so free from ambiguity that it may be evident on what foundation our hopes are built. When they who fear the Lord distinctly see that all our expectations are from Him, they will rejoice in our godly intercourse.

75. " *I know, O Lord, that Thy judgments are right, and that Thou in faithfulness hast afflicted me.*"

When afflictions oppress us it is well to remember the smiting hand. Correction is ordered in the Covenant for us. God in these trials acts in accordance with most holy rectitude.

76. " *Let, I pray Thee, Thy merciful kindness be for my comfort, according to Thy word unto Thy servant.*"

We often need strong consolation. A rich store is laid up for us in our God. To Him let us draw near and pray that all His promises to us in Christ Jesus may be our rich enjoyment.

*77. " Let Thy tender mercies come unto me, that I may
live : for Thy law is my delight."*

Tender mercy can prolong our days; but continued
life should only be desired in submission to God's will,
and for the furtherance of His glory. Such will be our
desire when our delight is to follow His law as our one
rule.

*78. " Let the proud be ashamed; for they dealt per-
versely with me without a cause; but I will meditate in
Thy precepts."*

Confusion will overwhelm the perverse adversaries.
Their persecution is without cause. Harmless will be
all their rage when the mind retires into the secret
places of holy meditation.

*79. " Let those that fear Thee turn unto me, and those
that have known Thy testimonies."*

The man of God delights only in the fellowship of
those who are fellow-servants of His God. They are
described as fearing God and intelligently keeping His
testimonies. Prayer is made that such may cheer him
by their company.

*80. " Let my heart be sound in Thy statutes, that I be
not ashamed."*

Let us ever be watchful over the treachery of our
hearts. They are prone to nurture unwholesome desires. But deviation from God's law brings shame.
Let us shun it as sure misery. Holiness may boldly
raise the head.

LXIV.

PSALM CXIX. 81–88.

81. "*My soul fainteth for Thy salvation; but I hope in Thy word.*"

Intense was the Psalmist's desire to realize an interest in God's salvation. Through anxiety he fails in strength, as a hart panting for the waterbrooks. But in weakness hope cheered him. Let us strive for an increase of this precious grace. It will gladden and sustain us.

82. "*Mine eyes fail for Thy word, saying, When wilt Thou comfort me?*"

If comforts seem to tarry long, the eye strained by constant looking becomes weak. Earnest cries wrestle with God for His restoring presence. The sigh is heard, How long shall trouble last? When will Thy comforts again revive me?

83. "*For I am become like a bottle in the smoke; yet do I not forget Thy statutes.*"

Under the grievous pressure of this trial, the bodily appearance manifests distress. The shrivelled skin loses all sign of moisture. It is dried like a leathern vessel in the smoke. But grace still lives and feasts on the banquet of God's word.

84. "*How many are the days of Thy servant? when wilt Thou execute judgment on them that persecute me?*"

It is sad when impatient peevishness frets. May the gracious Lord preserve us from such weakness!

Under its influence cessation of life is desired; vengeance calls for wrath on the head of persecutors. This is our infirmity. May the Lord pardon it and tear it from our hearts !

85. " *The proud have digged pits for me, which are not after Thy law.*"

Haughty persecutors may plot evil against the Lord's·followers. Such conduct is enmity to His law. Assuredly it will end in misery.

86. " *All Thy commandments are faithful: they persecute me wrongfully; help Thou me.*"

In such trial it is sweet relief to remember that God is true. According to the faithful Word, help will be given, and the persecutors perish in their wickedness.

87. " *They had almost consumed me upon earth: but I forsook not Thy precepts.*"

At times their cruel plans seem to border on success. Let not the righteous be dismayed. Let the Word be remembered which can never fail.

88. " *Quicken me after Thy loving-kindness; so shall I keep the testimony of Thy mouth.*"

Let prayer be made that God, in the multitude of His loving-kindness, would infuse new life into our drooping hearts. Then upright walking in the Lord's ways will not flag.

LXV.

PSALM CXIX. 89–96.

89. " For ever, O Lord, Thy word is settled in heaven."

Before the foundations of the world, the purposes of God were firmly settled. As He is stable and immutable, so they cannot change. Hence floods of peace and trust pervade the believer's heart. Every event flies on the wings of eternal decree.

90. " Thy faithfulness is unto all generations: Thou hast established the earth, and it abideth."

From age to age God's faithfulness shines in unfading brightness. The earth abides in accordance with original design. There is no interruption in its progress. It pursues the course of immutability.

91. " They continue this day according to thine ordinances: for all are Thy servants."

The course of nature undergoes no departure from primeval will. All things act out the great Creator's plan. His word commands perpetual obedience.

92. " Unless Thy law had been my delights, I should then have perished in mine affliction."

Afflictions often threaten to overwhelm. Billows upon billows go over the sinking head. But the immutable Word is grasped, and it is found to be a never-failing plank.

93. " I will never forget Thy precepts: for with them Thou hast quickened me."

It is our highest wisdom tightly to grasp the Word.

Let us set its precepts continually before our eyes. They are life-giving and life-sustaining. Let us enshrine them in our memories.

94. "*I am Thine, save me: for I have sought Thy precepts.*"

It is a happy moment when the believer can appeal to God, I am Thine. Thou hast called me, and I have obeyed. Thou hast quickened me, and I live to Thee. All my desire is to know and obey Thy will. Therefore I cry unto Thee for aid; save me, for I am Thy servant.

95. "*The wicked have waited for me to destroy me: but I will consider Thy testimonies.*"

I have indeed my foes. Plots are laid for my destruction. But I will not fear. The assurances of Thy Word sustain me.

96. "*I have seen an end of all perfection: but Thy commandment is exceeding broad.*"

Many objects are full of wonder. They excite admiration. But their beauty is not durable; it quickly fades away. But the glory of God's law suffers no eclipse. The more we ponder, the more cause shall we find for trust and praise.

LXVI.

PSALM CXIX. 97–104.

97. " *O how love I Thy law ! it is my meditation all the day.*"

Mark the profession of the blessed man. Every affection goes forth in admiration of the law. It is his constant delight. At every moment of the day his heart lovingly feasts on it.

98. " *Thou, through Thy commandments, hast made me wiser than mine enemies ; for they are ever with me.*"

Where can true wisdom be found but in the counsels of the all-wise and only-wise God ! His name and His word are emphatic wisdom. They are the perfection of intelligence. They ever fill the believer's heart. Thus his foes appear as fools before him.

99. " *I have more understanding than all my teachers : for Thy testimonies are my meditation.*"

The world professes to have schools of sage instruction ; but the poorest believer, enlightened by the Spirit, is wiser than this boasted wisdom. God's testimonies are his meditation. Hence he derives celestial understanding.

100. " *I understand more than the ancients, because I keep Thy precepts.*"

The lowliest man who has the Bible in his heart knows more than the sage philosophers of old. True wisdom is acquired in the path of heavenly precepts.

101. " *I have refrained my feet from every evil way, that I might keep Thy word.*"

The blessed man maintains an undeviating course of godliness. Let us diligently mark the perilous way of evil. Let us flee from it as from a pitfall. So shall we keep the path of safety and pure joy.

102. "*I have not departed from Thy judgments: for Thou hast taught me.*"

Unless we are apt pupils in God's school we shall not clearly see the heavenward road, and quickly shall we be beguiled by error's snares. It is a happy profession, Thou hast taught me. It may be added, Therefore I am above the reach of harm.

103. "*How sweet are Thy words unto my taste! yea, sweeter than honey to my mouth!*"

They who make the law their constant feast find in it delicious relish. The heart is more refreshed than the palate can be by the sweetest luxury that nature knows.

104. "*Through Thy precepts I get understanding: therefore I hate every false way.*"

It is a solid truth that understanding is obtained by diligent adherence to God's precepts. The sure result is hatred of all false ways. May the Lord teach us, and cause us to walk in truth!

LXVII.

PSALM CXIX. 105—112.

105. " *Thy word is a lamp unto my feet, and a light unto my path.*"

Our path is often through a cloudy land. Safe guidance is provided in the Word. They who hold this lamp shall not walk in darkness, but shall have the light of life. It will lead to the home in which there is no need of the sun or of the moon to lighten, but the Lord is the light thereof.

106. " *I have sworn, and I will perform it, that I will keep Thy righteous judgments.*"

All means should be employed to bind us to unbroken obedience. The vows by which we are consecrated to God's service should stand as a barrier against every straying step. God's covenant of grace is confirmed by oath. Thus, too, should our holy walk be ratified.

107. " *I am afflicted very much: quicken me, O Lord, according unto Thy word.*"

When afflictions press heavily, the surest relief arises from earnest prayer. Let our petition be for insight into the life-imparting Word.

108. " *Accept, I beseech Thee, the free-will-offerings of my mouth, O Lord, and teach me Thy judgments.*"

We should present ourselves, our every faculty and power as a whole burnt-offering to the Lord. But especially, we should bring the calves of our lips. The sacrifice of prayer and praise should never cease.

May the Lord of His free grace accept our service! May it be perfumed by the incense of Christ's blood! In this exercise may we advance in heavenly knowledge!

109. "*My soul is continually in my hand: yet do I not forget Thy law.*"

The believer counts not his life dear unto himself, so that he may finish his course with joy. He is always in the very jaws of death. He lives with wings outstretched to fly away. Paul testified: I die daily. In the extremity of persecution, the fervent desire was to know what God would have him to do.

110. "*The wicked have laid a snare for me; yet I erred not from Thy precepts.*"

No plots of the ungodly can compel deviation from God's law. The right way may seem to be beset with perils, but let it be resolutely chosen. Its end is happiness and peace.

111. "*Thy testimonies have I taken as an heritage for ever: for they are the rejoicing of my heart.*"

The possession of God's truth is an inalienable treasure. It enriches with possessions which never can decay, and which no spoiler can remove. It fills with joy unspeakable. It leads to endless glory.

112. "*I have inclined mine heart to perform Thy statutes alway, even unto the end.*"

It is true that God only can incline the heart, but when He works converting change, adherence to God's will seems to be easy service. It becomes the spontaneous effort of the mind. May we thus find that obedience is our ready pathway to the glorious end, which has no end!

LXVIII.

PSALM CXIX. 113-120.

113. "*I hate vain thoughts: but Thy law do I love.*"

Universal is the corruption implanted by the fall. Every imagination is prone to evil continually. The believer is conscious of this, and deeply bewails. The vanity of his thoughts is regarded with intense hatred. His real love is given to the pure Word.

114. "*Thou art my hiding-place and my shield: I hope in Thy word.*"

The believer has a high fortress in his God. He flees to this hiding-place, and is safe. When the arrows of the foe unsparingly assail, he finds protection under the shield of God. He faints not, for his hope in God is firm.

115. "*Depart from me, ye evil-doers: for I will keep the commandments of my God.*"

The presence of evil men gives keen distress. The believer strives to keep far apart, and to give himself wholly to the works of godliness.

116. "*Uphold me according unto Thy word, that I may live: and let me not be ashamed of my hope.*"

Our natural strength is utter feebleness. Unless upheld by a heavenly arm, we cannot but fall. But we may plead the promises. Thus we continue in lively frame. Thus the head looks up in holy confidence.

117. "*Hold Thou me up, and I shall be safe: and I will have respect unto Thy statutes continually.*"

There is no safety unless the Lord extends support. May our strength be thus supplied! This help will secure adherence to God's statutes.

118. " *Thou hast trodden down all them that err from Thy statutes : for their deceit is falsehood.*"

They cannot escape ruin who wander in devious paths. Divine vengeance is in their rear. They will soon be trampled into perdition. Deceit and falsehood have been their course. The end is misery.

119. " *Thou puttest away all the wicked of the earth like dross: therefore I love Thy testimonies.*"

Utterly worthless are the wicked. They are lighter than the worthless chaff. The Lord will drive them away. They will no more be seen. They are the blessed who take His testimonies for their enriching treasure.

120. " *My flesh trembleth for fear of Thee ; and I am afraid of Thy judgments.*"

Who can think of the majesty and glory of God, and not lie low in reverential awe! The contemplation of His righteous judgments is an appalling sight, for an angry God is a consuming fire. Blessed are they who are sheltered in Christ Jesus.

LXIX.

PSALM CXIX. 121-128.

121. *"I have done judgment and justice: leave me not to mine oppressors."*

Happy is the conscience which can testify of sincere effort to act uprightly. Such walk leads to protection. Divine grace will uphold. Then the prayer may truly go forth, Leave me not to oppression, I have striven never to oppress.

122. *"Be surety for Thy servant for good: let not the proud oppress me."*

In the provisions of grace God is engaged to uphold His servants, to avert evil, and to rescue them from oppression. Let the humble pleading go forth, Deal with me according to the everlasting Covenant.

123. *"Mine eyes fail for Thy salvation, and for the word of Thy righteousness."*

Believers long with intense desire to realize the joys of salvation. Their eyes are strained in looking for the shining of God's righteous word upon their hearts.

124. *"Deal with Thy servant according unto Thy mercy, and teach me Thy statutes."*

In deep confession of misery faith looks for help only from God's mercy. This mercy never fails. It has no bounds. It never can be sought in vain. Its work is to guide safely in the way of heavenly statutes.

125. *"I am Thy servant; give me understanding, that I may know Thy testimonies."*

It is happiness to draw near to God with humble profession, that He is the Lord to whose service we are willingly consecrated. This is a good plea for light from heaven to direct our paths.

126. "*It is time for Thee, Lord, to work; for they have made void Thy law.*"

When iniquity abounds, and God's law is utterly despised, the time is come for God to arise, and to maintain His own cause. Let us give Him no rest until He banishes all evil.

127. "*Therefore I love Thy commandments above gold, yea, above fine gold.*"

What are all the treasures of earth beside the precious Word of God! The believer knows its value, and he regards all earth's wealth as worthless in comparison.

128. "*Therefore I esteem all Thy precepts concerning all things to be right: and I hate every false way.*"

Admiration of God's law should be universal. Every precept should be regarded as a direct voice from heaven. Every opposing word should be rejected as falsehood and deception. May this be the mould in which our hearts are framed!

LXX.

PSALM CXIX. 129–136.

129. "*Thy testimonies are wonderful: therefore doth my soul keep them.*"

Wonderful, indeed, are the revelations of Scripture. They proclaim Him whose name is Wonderful, and Who only doeth wondrous things. The more this Word is studied the stronger will be the effort that the whole life should be framed after its sacred model.

130. "*The entrance of Thy words giveth light; it giveth understanding unto the simple.*"

The fall extinguished spiritual light. Gross darkness beclouded the mind. But when the rays of the Word illumine, bright intelligence sees God and the way of life. How earnest should be the prayer, "Send out Thy light and Thy truth, that they may lead me!" Thus the simple obtain wisdom.

131. "*I opened my mouth and panted: for I longed for Thy commandments.*"

Man gasping by toil and heat is pictured. He pants for the refreshing breeze. Thus the believer thirsts for the reviving comfort of God's Word.

132. "*Look Thou upon me, and be merciful unto me, as Thou usest to do unto those that love Thy name.*"

God's tender mercies ever beam on those who love Him. The Psalmist professes that such is his state, and prays to be remembered in the household of the saints.

133. "*Order my steps in Thy word: and let not any iniquity have dominion over me.*"

It is the believer's constant desire that God would guide his footsteps. He hates iniquity, and prays to be delivered from its thraldom.

134. "*Deliver me from the oppression of man: so will I keep Thy precepts.*"

Unless the Lord sends help, cruel men will terribly oppress the godly. But upheld by Him, they will persevere in the righteous precepts.

135. "*Make Thy face to shine upon Thy servant; and teach me Thy statutes.*"

Blessed is the state when heavenly smiles shine sweetly on the heart. This is the very foretaste of the heaven of heavens. They who enjoy these cheering rays will always long to profit in God's school.

136. "*Rivers of waters run down mine eyes, because they keep not Thy law.*"

Keen is the pain when the godly see God's name profaned, His Word despised, His glory trampled beneath contemning feet. Pious feeling mourns. Streams of sorrow show the intense anguish. Love of God awakens grief when He is contemned. May we know this holy sorrow!

LXXI.

PSALM CXIX. 137-144.

137. "*Righteous art Thou, O Lord, and upright are Thy judgments.*"

It is supreme delight to contemplate the glories of holiness, which, as a halo, shine around our Lord. God is holy in all His attributes and works.

138. "*Thy testimonies that Thou hast commanded are righteous and very faithful.*"

Every commandment is the essence of holiness. His every word is the splendour of truth. Let the Scriptures be our constant guide. They will sanctify, and mould the inner man in righteousness.

139. "*My zeal hath consumed me; because mine enemies have forgotten Thy words.*"

Strong feelings are excited in the godly breast when disregard of God's Word is seen. It is the actuating principle of His enemies. The righteous burn with zeal to check it.

140. "*Thy word is very pure: therefore Thy servant loveth it.*"

The lovely purity of God's Word is wondrous to attract. The godly feel this influence, and delight in it with their whole hearts.

141. "*I am small and despised; yet do not I forget Thy precepts.*"

The godly know well their poverty. They often feel that the world regards them with contempt. But these feelings excite warmer desire to be conformed to the Word of God.

142. " *Thy righteousness is an everlasting righteousness, and Thy law is the truth.*"

God's righteousness is exact conformity to His law. The blessed Jesus, in man's nature upon earth, exhibited this righteousness. It is the robe which secures admission into heaven. It is everlasting, and incapable of change or decay.

143. " *Trouble and anguish have taken hold on me; yet Thy commandments are my delights.*"

Man is born to trouble, as the sparks fly upward; but no affliction drives the believer from the law which he intensely loves.

144. " *The righteousness of Thy testimonies is everlasting: give me understanding, and I shall live.*"

God's law is immutable. No age brings change. Fully persuaded of this truth, the believer prays to be kept in its knowledge. It leads to eternal life. May it be our chosen guide!

LXXII.

PSALM CXIX. 145–152.

145. "*I cried with my whole heart; hear me, O Lord: I will keep Thy statutes.*"

Prayer and profession are here combined. Sweet is the union. May they ever be conjoined in us! True prayer is an exercise in which the whole heart puts forth its utmost energy. Prayers should be heartfelt vows.

146. "*I cried unto Thee; save me, and I shall keep Thy testimonies.*"

Faith looks back hopefully on the hours in which prayer has been urgent. It supplicates anew for God's saving hand. It resolves to render faithful service in return.

147. "*I prevented the dawning of the morning, and cried: I hoped in Thy word.*"

Faith is impatient to reach the mercy-seat. Before the first rays enlighten the east, it hastens to its morning work of prayer. Its hope rests on the promises of the Word.

148. "*Mine eyes prevent the night watches, that I might meditate in Thy word.*"

Before the evening shadows darken, it hastens again to the glad employ of holy meditation. Stillness aids the calm delight.

149. "*Hear my voice according unto Thy loving-kindness: O Lord, quicken me according to Thy judgment.*"

The views of God's loving-kindness are incessant joy. Faith expects much. Its hopes are large, according to the measure of God's goodness.

150. "*They draw nigh that follow after mischief: they are far from Thy law.*"

Plotters of mischief against God's servants are always near. They hate God's law. We here read the complaint of Jesus. But all malice came to nought.

151. "*Thou art near, O Lord; and all Thy commandments are truth.*"

The workers of mischief are indeed near, but God is far nearer. His presence is granted according to His promises.

152. "*Concerning Thy testimonies, I have known of old that Thou hast founded them for ever.*"

It is the immovable persuasion of faith that no word of God's mouth can ever fail. The soul is happy which reposes on this rock. May it be our settled resting-place!

LXXIII.

PSALM CXIX. 153-160.

153. "*Consider mine affliction, and deliver me ; for I do not forget Thy law.*"

It is our privilege to bring afflictions to the mercy-seat. God is always ready to give ear. Relief will not long tarry. Happy is it when we can add the plea that His law rules within us.

154. "*Plead my cause, and deliver me: quicken me according to Thy word.*"

All our adversaries are silenced, when our great Advocate appears on our behalf. We may boldly pray, when we seek only the fulfilment of the Covenant of grace.

155. "*Salvation is far from the wicked : for they seek not Thy statutes.*"

Sure is the destruction of the ungodly. Vengeance, righteously denounced, will righteously be executed. Where can hope be found ? God's statutes are rejected. Self-willed rebellion fights only that it may fall.

156. "*Great are Thy tender mercies, O Lord: quicken me according to Thy judgments.*"

The tender mercies of our God exceed all powers to estimate and praise. We need more love in our hearts. Our affections should more warmly burn. Let earnest prayers invigorate our souls. He giveth more grace.

157. "*Many are my persecutors and mine enemies;
yet do I not decline from Thy testimonies.*"

Vain is all the rage and malice of the ungodly when
God extends His protecting shield. When the enemy
comes in like a flood, may we adhere more steadfastly
to the rock of our salvation!

158. "*I beheld the transgressors, and was grieved; because they kept not Thy word.*"

An ungodly man is the saddest sight on earth. His
course is unmixed evil. None gain profit from him.
He passes to endless misery. Who can behold and
suppress sorrow! This misery results from neglect of
God's Word.

159. "*Consider how I love Thy precepts: quicken me,
O Lord, according to Thy loving-kindness.*"

Happy are they who with pure conscience can call
on God to behold their devoted attachment to His
Word. But still they bewail their dull and lifeless
state, and pray for quickening power.

160. "*Thy word is true from the beginning: and
every one of Thy righteous judgments endureth for ever.*"

Truth reigns in every word of Scripture. Its first
utterance was true. This property will pervade it to
the end. Let this thought quicken our delight in it.
It never can mislead. It will abide God's truth through
everlasting ages.

LXXIV.

PSALM CXIX. 161–168.

161. "*Princes have persecuted me without a cause: but my heart standeth in awe of Thy word.*"

Exaltation to earth's greatness cannot raise the soul to sanctity. The kings of the earth have often been among the foremost to take counsel against the Lord, and against His Anointed. Such conduct is extreme infatuation. But the godly fear not. They who stand in awe of God can lightly regard man.

162. "*I rejoice at Thy word, as one that findeth great spoil.*"

The Word of God is the treasure of treasures. It makes wise unto salvation. It enriches with imperishable wealth. Shall the man rejoice who discovers earthly spoils, and shall he not rejoice who finds the pearl of great price!

163. "*I hate and abhor lying: but Thy law do I love.*"

Truth is a pure and lovely grace. Let us regard with detestation every deviation from the paths of truth. Let us give our hearts to the law, which is God's truth in the highest.

164. "*Seven times a day do I praise Thee because of Thy righteous judgments.*"

No praise can suffice to give due adoration to the Lord. Let His praises ever be on our lips. In His righteous judgments we shall find unending theme.

165. "*Great peace have they which love Thy law: and nothing shall offend them.*"

What can disturb the calm tranquillity of those whose affections revel in the Word of God! They proceed on earth's journey safely; nothing can cause them to fall fatally.

166. *"Lord, I have hoped for Thy salvation, and done Thy commandments."*

Here we have the sweet profession of established faith. It rejoices in the full assurance of hope, that God's salvation is its possession. In this glad persuasion the life is conformed to strictest obedience.

167. *"My soul hath kept Thy testimonies; and I love them exceedingly."*

The path of godliness is exceeding joy. The more we walk in it the more will delight abound.

168. *"I have kept Thy precepts and Thy testimonies: for all my ways are before Thee."*

The believer ever realizes that God sees him. He would not that any word or work were hidden from his Heavenly Father. May we ever walk in the bright sunshine of His light! Let us call Him to be our constant witness.

LXXV.

PSALM CXIX. 169-176.

169. *" Let my cry come near before Thee, O Lord: give me understanding according to Thy word."*

The believer's life is prayer. His faith assures him that every supplication will be heard. He feels especially his ignorance. Hence he seeks wisdom from God, who giveth liberally and upbraideth not.

170. *" Let my supplication come before Thee; deliver me according to Thy word."*

The prayer is often repeated that in gracious answer deliverance may come. He trusts in the Covenant of grace.

171. *" My lips shall utter praise, when Thou hast taught me Thy statutes."*

Strong is the desire that due praises may be rendered. Hence the constant prayer that heavenly intelligence may be vouchsafed.

172. *" My tongue shall speak of Thy word: for all Thy commandments are righteousness."*

Sweet is the converse when God's Word is the theme. How worthless in comparison are the chatterings of earthly folly!

173. *" Let Thine hand help me: for I have chosen Thy precepts."*

Strong is the plea: Lord, Thou knowest that deliberately I choose Thy way. We may then boldly ask for help, and help will quickly fly to our side.

174. "*I have longed for Thy salvation, O Lord ; and Thy law is my delight.*"

Happy is Jacob's testimony, "I have waited for Thy salvation." David similarly professed, "I have longed for Thy salvation." Such saints have great delights. Their joy flows from the Word of God.

175. "*Let my soul live, and it shall praise Thee ; and let Thy judgments help me.*"

Liveliness of soul is the Spirit's gift, and it will show itself in abounding praises.

176. "*I have gone astray like a lost sheep: seek Thy servant ; for I do not forget Thy commandments.*"

The experienced saint is always conscious of his frequent errings. Unless the Good Shepherd seeks the straying sheep, it will wander farther from the fold. Hence prayer is made to God to restore the soul from devious paths. This prayer is enforced by the profession that God's commandments abide in the heart.

LXXVI.

PSALM CXX.

THIS Psalm depicts the unhappy condition when calumnies assail, and the soul is tossed on billows of disquietude. Prayer is the unfailing refuge.

———

1. "*In my distress I cried unto the Lord, and He heard me.*"

Scripture faithfully proclaims that much tribulation is the believer's lot in this world. But it stops not with a mournful note. It also reveals the remedy in every period of distress. The remedy is prayer. This exercise never fails to bring relief. A distinct example stands before us. The Psalmist, mourning in the depths of trouble, lifts up a supplicating voice. God's ears are graciously open. We shall have sorrow. Let us similarly cry, and we shall find that sorrow leads to joy.

2. "*Deliver my soul, O Lord, from lying lips, and from a deceitful tongue.*"

A particular distress is now named. The exact petition is adjoined. Calumny and untruthful reports constitute the trial. The believer is often called to this endurance. If David is the speaker, we hear him mourning the cruel charge of Doeg. If the blessed Jesus is the prominent personage, we know that things were laid to His charge which He knew not of. But when-

ever such cruelty occurs, God is a sure refuge.   No
bitter arrow wounds when His shield shelters.

3, 4. " *What shall be given unto thee? or what shall be
done unto thee, thou false tongue?   Sharp arrows of the
mighty, with coals of juniper.*"

Expostulation is made with the slandering accuser.
He is warned that he cannot expect immunity.   God
will vindicate His children.   He will bring fierce destruction on malignant calumniators.   Images vividly
express the terrible aspect of this punishment.   Miseries
shall pierce false hearts, as arrows flying from a mighty
bow.   Fire shall consume them, as the fierce coals of
juniper.

5. " *Woe is me, that I sojourn in Mesech, that I dwell
in the tents of Kedar!*"

Here is a lamentation that abode so long continues
in the midst of the cruel and idolatrous.   Let us seek
more the sweet communion of saints.   Let us long
more for the fellowship of heaven, where love shall be
the pervading atmosphere, and praise the never-ending
song.

6, 7. " *My soul hath long dwelt with him that hateth
peace.   I am for peace; but when I speak, they are for
war.*"

If the blessed Jesus found such to be His case, can
His followers expect a better state!   But let us never
be provoked to render evil for evil, but contrariwise
blessing.   Let us pray that the God of peace may give
us peace, always and by all means.

LXXVII.

PSALM CXXI.

TRUE safety is from God alone. His protecting care is portrayed in attractive colours. May they win us to place all confidence in Him!

1, 2. *"I will lift up mine eyes unto the hills, from whence cometh my help. My help cometh from the Lord, which made heaven and earth."*

The pious child of Israel turned in devotion to the hill on which the Temple stood. He saw in it a type of Jehovah's presence. The lesson is here taught that all protection comes directly from our Heavenly Father. With confidence let us uplift our eyes to Him. He is the fountain of all grace. He, whose omnipotent word called heaven and earth into existence, can by the same word make all providences to subserve His people's good.

3, 4. *"He will not suffer thy foot to be moved: He that keepeth thee will not slumber. Behold, He that keepeth Israel shall neither slumber nor sleep."*

The believer often moves on slippery ground. Various enemies, too, dash against him. Left to himself, how quickly will he fall! But the Lord upholds him; so he stands as a rock against the lashing billows. The care which preserves him never remits its watchful guardianship. The eyes of the Lord, through day and night, from the opening to the closing of the year, are fixed immovably on His waiting people.

5, 6. "*The Lord is thy keeper; the Lord is thy shade upon thy right hand. The sun shall not smite thee by day, nor the moon by night.*"

Volumes are contained in the words, The Lord is thy keeper. It is re-echoed by the Apostle—We are kept by the power of God through faith unto eternal life. They are indeed securely kept who are encircled by their omnipotent God. In their Zionward march they are exposed to scorching rays. But as the pillar of cloud spread sweet refreshment over Israel's hosts, so the Lord wards off the adversary's piercing darts. To His people He is as the shadow of a great rock in a weary land.

7. "*The Lord shall preserve thee from all evil; He shall preserve thy soul.*"

All strength and joy are included in the promise that God shall preserve us from all evil. The believer may exult in the assurance that all the assaults of Satan and the powers of darkness shall inflict no deadly wound. The soul shall live unharmed. It shall be brought in safety to the heavenly home.

8. "*The Lord shall preserve thy going out, and thy coming in, from this time forth, and even for evermore.*"

The pilgrimage may seem tedious. We may have many changes. We may be emptied from vessel to vessel. But final rest is secured. Through God's protection, heaven shall be attained. Let us lift up our heads with joy, and shout thanksgivings.

LXXVIII.

PSALM CXXII.

THE beauty and the glory of the Church of Christ are here typically represented. Let prayer be fervent for the Church.

1, 2. "*I was glad when they said unto me, Let us go into the house of the Lord. Our feet shall stand within thy gates, O Jerusalem !*"

Joy gladdened the Israelite's heart when invited to proceed in happy company to the appointed worship at Jerusalem. He would rejoice in the hope of seeing the royal city and the Temple of his God. His spirit would exult in prospect of joining in the prayers and praises of the sanctuary. Gladness would largely revel when he exclaimed, Our feet shall stand within thy gates, O Jerusalem! Similar is the pious joy with which every true believer hastens to the Church's festivities. It is celestial happiness to join in common prayer, to lift up the voice in common praise, and to hear the proclamation of the glorious truths of Christ's gospel. But what lips can tell the joy of entering the New Jerusalem; and seeing our God face to face, and joining in the everlasting hallelujahs! With this bright prospect gladdening our souls may we go on our way rejoicing!

3. "*Jerusalem is builded as a city that is compact together.*"

Nothing could exceed the magnificence of the city of God. It abounded with all that art and wealth could contribute. Thus it stood the admiration of the world. Its perfect arrangements present a faint image of the glory of the New Jerusalem. The Spirit, by the pen of the enraptured John, describes the glorious scene. But splendid images cannot reach the reality. To know what heaven is, heaven must be entered. May we rejoice in the thought that each day brings us nearer to it!

4, 5. "*Whither the tribes go up, the tribes of the Lord, unto the testimony of Israel, to give thanks unto the name of the Lord. For there are set thrones of judgment, the thrones of the house of David.*"

Thrice in each year the males of the house of Israel were enjoined to attend the solemn feasts, to enter the Temple, which contained the testimony of the Lord, and there to bless His holy name. The day approaches when all who have rejoiced in Christ shall meet in the New Jerusalem. They shall come from the east and from the west, from the north and from the south, with joy and gladness, with thanksgiving, and the voice of melody. Let us see to it that we, too, shall have our place in this innumerable multitude. Believers are kings and priests now unto God. Then shall the promise be fulfilled, I say unto you, That ye which have followed Me, in the regeneration when the Son of man shall sit on the throne of His glory, ye also shall sit upon twelve thrones, judging the twelve tribes of Israel.

6, 7. "*Pray for the peace of Jerusalem: they shall prosper that love thee. Peace be within thy walls, and prosperity within thy palaces.*"

We are exhorted to be constant in our prayers, that God's choicest blessings may descend upon the Church and meeten it for the inheritance of glory. Prayers for others are true prayers for ourselves. When we seek mercy on the Church in general, mercy will be vouchsafed to us, as to all the members of it.

8, 9, "*For my brethren and companions' sakes, I will now say, Peace be within thee. Because of the house of the Lord our God I will seek thy good.*"

Two grand motives are assigned for these prayers, the love of our brethren and our delight in the glory of God. May these motives ever swell in our hearts. Asking peace for others, we shall enjoy peace ourselves. If we honour God, He will honour us.

LXXIX.

PSALM CXXIII.

CONTEMPT and derision should quicken our flight to the mercy-seat.

1. " *Unto Thee lift I up mine eyes, O Thou that dwellest in the heavens.*"

The Psalmist holds in his hand a cup overflowing with bitter waters of distress. But he knows from whom relief can be obtained. He looks away—He looks aloft—He looks on high—He looks to the heaven of heavens—He looks to his God and Father in Christ Jesus. High indeed is His glorious throne, but the eye of faith can reach it. It sees seated thereon His Father invested with all plenitude of power, and beaming with all smiles of love. Let us fear no trouble, which brings us to this light.

2. " *Behold, as the eyes of servants look unto the hand of their masters, and as the eyes of a maiden unto the hand of her mistress; so our eyes wait upon the Lord our God, until that He have mercy upon us.*"

A homely similitude shows the intense and patient watchings of faith. The devoted servant diligently observes his master. He studies to learn his will. His desire is to execute his wishes. So faith is ever studious to ascertain what God would have us to do. It looks upward, not doubting that God will guide with

His eye.   Faith, too, is very patient.   It humbly waits
until mercy is vouchsafed.   He who thus watches
will surely find that mercy in due time will radiantly
shine forth.

3, 4.   " *Have mercy upon us, O Lord, have mercy upon
us ; for we are exceedingly filled with contempt.   Our soul
is exceedingly filled with the scorning of those that are at
ease, and with the contempt of the proud.*"

The cry for mercy is strong and importunate.   It
will not cease until mercy's wings flutter around.   It
is especially urged by the contemptuous bearing of the
ungodly.   They scornfully deride the humble followers
of the Lamb.   But great will be the change, when the
proud are cast into outer darkness, and the lowly raised
to their eternal thrones.   Let us·be the true followers
of the meek and lowly Jesus, that we may dwell with
Him for ever.

LXXX.

PSALM CXXIV.

ALL deliverance is freely given by the hand of God. To
Him let grateful blessings ever be ascribed.

1, 2, 3, 4, 5. *" If it had not been the Lord who was on
our side, now may Israel say ; If it had not been the Lord
who was on our side, when men rose up against us : then
they had swallowed us up quick, when their wrath was
kindled against us : then the waters had overwhelmed us,
the stream had gone over our soul : then the proud waters
had gone over our soul."*

Many are the adversaries of God's children. They
are headed by the arch-enemy the devil. He is depicted as a lion for strength, a serpent for subtlety, a
dragon for fierceness. He is aided by followers who are
a legion for multitude. Tender feeling is a stranger to
such foes. Like the waters of an overwhelming flood,
they would work utter desolation. Their malice must
succeed, if One mightier than the strong one interposed
not. But the Lord is ever near to succour His people.
Vain is all hostility. His aid is perfect victory.

6. *" Blessed be the Lord, who hath not given us as a
prey to their teeth."*

The soul is represented as a defenceless lamb trembling in the fangs of a ravenous beast, ready to mangle,
eager to devour. But rescue intervenes. So our

Heavenly Father delivers from the teeth of the devour-ing lion. Let grateful thanks be devoutly given.

7. *" Our soul is escaped as a bird out of the snare of the fowlers: the snare is broken, and we are escaped."*

Another image represents the soul entangled in the fowler's net. A kind hand brings escape. When the case seems to be hopeless, mercy gives freedom. Again let praises shout aloud.

8. *" Our help is in the name of the Lord, who made heaven and earth."*

Surely we must perish if earth only rendered aid. But the great Creator who sits on the throne of omni-potence puts forth His might in our defence. This power is an impregnable fortress of defence. Let us thank Him, bless Him, and adore.

LXXXI.

PSALM CXXV.

THIS ode sings a blessed description of God's children. Earnest prayer is the fit conclusion.

———————

1. " *They that trust in the Lord shall be as Mount Zion, which cannot be removed, but abideth for ever.*"

It is the blessing of blessings to put all trust in God. They who thus cling to Him shall never be cast off. Perils may environ them, but hostile might shall not prevail. As easily might puny man cast down the loftiest mountains as adverse power shake the firm stability of this faith. May this trust nerve us in the Christian warfare !

2. " *As the mountains are round about Jerusalem, so the Lord is round about His people from henceforth, even for ever.*"

Jerusalem was guarded by natural barriers. Surrounding mountains spread protecting arms. This image shows the safety of God's people. On all sides He stands their sure protection. He must be removed or vanquished before an adversary can touch them. Our life is hid with Christ in God. Can safety be more safe ?

3. " *For the rod of the wicked shall not rest upon the lot of the righteous ; lest the righteous put forth their hands unto iniquity.*"

Hostile might may often rage against the righteous. Foes may threaten to trample them beneath their feet. But God will check the overbearing enmity. If trials should long prevail there might be peril, lest the spirits of the righteous should faint. Fear of desertion might open the door to many doubts. But all such danger is averted by the hand of God. His ready help restores confiding hope.

4. "*Do good, O Lord, unto those that be good, and to them that are upright in their hearts.*"

Believers are described as good. The name is explained by the Spirit as implying the indwelling of the Holy Ghost and of faith. It is proof that no guile is harboured in their hearts. Prayer is made that God would visit them with goodness. This prayer indited by the Spirit amounts to a heavenly promise that they shall receive such honour.

5. "*As for such as turn aside unto their crooked ways, the Lord shall lead them forth with the workers of iniquity: but peace shall be upon Israel.*"

Transition of scene shows the deceitful followers of evil led forth by God to merited execution, while the true Israel rejoice in abundant peace. May this happy state be our glad portion! Grant it, Heavenly Father, for Thy love's sake, in Christ Jesus!

LXXXII.

PSALM CXXVI.

RESTORATION from captivity is the Lord's gracious work. In due time the sorrow of the righteous shall be swallowed up in joy.

------

1. " *When the Lord turned again the captivity of Zion, we were like them that dream.*"

When the days of Babylonish bondage were fully run, what transports of joy thrilled through Israel's sons! Their minds were almost bewildered by the grand event. The good tidings seemed almost as the mocking of an illusive vision of the night. So when deliverance from Satan's yoke is realized, what floods of delight overpower the soul! We were born captives in the devil's prison-house, his shackles held us tightly bound. We were slaves toiling under a cruel tyrant. But when Jesus comes and grants liberty we awake to a new world of happiness. We breathe the air of freedom. We exult with joy unspeakable and full of glory. We are tempted to exclaim, Can this be real!

2. " *Then was our mouth filled with laughter, and our tongue with singing: then said they among the heathen, The Lord hath done great things for them.*"

Their homeward march was lively with exuberant

thanksgiving. The voice of pious melody was heard around. The heathen beheld the marvellous return. At once they exclaimed that One mightier than man had come forth for their rescue. May we ever ascribe our redemption to free grace!

3. "*The Lord hath done great things for us, whereof we are glad.*"

The Lord, indeed, has done great things for us. Omnipotence has mightily come forth to save us from the grasp of Satan. Jesus, the incarnate God, has grappled with our deadly foe. He has snatched us from his thraldom. The great God brings salvation. Shall we not rejoice and sing!

4. "*Turn again our captivity, O Lord, as the streams in the south.*"

When the heat of summer burns, many torrents show dry channels. The cattle, thirsting for refreshing waters, are mocked with empty beds. But when the rains return, their channels are again replenished, and gladness smiles beside their banks. So when the days of banishment are passed, the captives move homeward with delight. May the Lord speedily bring this joy to those who groan beneath Satan's cruel yoke!

5, 6. "*They that sow in tears shall reap in joy. He that goeth forth and weepeth, bearing precious seed, shall doubtless come again with rejoicing, bringing his sheaves with him.*"

An image from rustic life gives comfort. The husbandman in hopeful toil casts the seed into the furrows. Months pass and there is no sign of life. In due season spring returns. The fields again are clad with verdure. Summer glows with ripening rays.

The harvest is gathered in amid full shouts of joy. So a long period of dreary waiting may depress the soul; but the promised deliverance comes, and sorrow flees in shouts of fervent joy. May this be speedily our glad experience!

LXXXIII.

PSALM CXXVII.

SAFETY and success can only come from God. Pious families are multiplied by His blessing.

---

1. "*Except the Lord build the house, they labour in vain that build it: except the Lord keep the city, the watchman waketh but in vain.*"

It is a blessed lesson in the Spirit's school that God's all-ordering hand and all-controlling power direct events. He sits upon the throne of universal sway. Prosperity abounds as furthered by His will. Failure undermines all efforts which rest not on His sovereign desire. All labour is but nothingness except He commands the blessing. Without Him workmen toil to gain vanity. Guards may surround the city with much show of force, but if the Lord be absent their arms and vigilance end in defeat. Jesus comforts with the assurance that all power is His in heaven and in earth. Let us flee to Him and cling to Him. Then we shall surely prosper. Adversity can never frown when Jesus smiles.

2. "*It is vain for you to rise up early, to sit up late, to eat the bread of sorrows: for so He giveth His beloved sleep.*"

It is sad when men consume their time and energies in fruitless toil. If God be forgotten, and His aid unsought, the midnight hours and the early dawn are

vainly spent in labours. Profitless is all exercise of mind
and body if He is excluded Who alone dispenses blessings. Shut out the sun, and there is no light. Omit
the ball, and empty is the cannon's sound. Let His
servants make Him their all, and He will cause them to
repose in peace. Tranquil confidence will trust events
to His guardian care, and thus sweet calm will soothe
the breast.

3, 4, 5. " *Lo, children are an heritage of the Lord: and
the fruit of the womb is His reward. As arrows are in
the hand of a mighty man ; so are children of the youth.
Happy is the man that hath his quiver full of them : they
shall not be ashamed, but they shall speak with the enemies
in the gate.*"

It is a lovely scene when pious parents sit surrounded
by a pious progeny. The happy circle gives evidence
that God's favouring smile beams on the family.
Heavenly feeling pervades the house. Love of God,
faith in the redeeming blood and covering righteousness
of Christ, are ruling principles. There is joy in present
intercourse and in anticipation of eternal fellowship.
The godly union, too, is strength. No enemies can
resist the arrows aimed by a giant hand. Thus foes
prevail not over this holy company. No shame or confusion depresses their heads. They boldly meet all
adversaries. Who will not serve the blessed Lord, and
delight in the heritage which is His people's crown !

LXXXIV.

PSALM CXXVIII.

MANIFOLD blessings belong to those who fear the Lord. May we gaze on the display until it is our own realized enjoyment!

———————

1. " *Blessed is every one that feareth the Lord; that walketh in His ways.*"

The fear of the Lord is an inestimable gift. Let it be sought with our whole hearts. Let it be diligently nurtured. It comes from above. It is the Spirit's work. It is the herald of a train of countless blessings. It is evidenced by close adherence to the Gospel-rule. They who fear God will dread the slightest wandering from His path.

2. " *For thou shalt eat the labour of thine hands: happy shalt thou be, and it shall be well with thee.*"

The grace of fear will work diligence in all appointed works. Indolence is a mark of gracelessness. Abundant fruit follows Christian toil. No good thing shall be withheld. True happiness fills the hearts which tremble at the Word. God will cause the sunshine of prosperity to brighten in their homes. Who will not pray, Lord, give us this blessed fear! As the heaven is high above the earth, so great is His mercy towards them that fear Him.

3. " *Thy wife shall be as a fruitful vine by the sides of*

thine house: thy children like olive-plants round about thy table."

Not only shall prosperity attend the customary employ of the hands, but domestic joys shall be dispensed as the Lord thinks well. His blessing will fill the cup of family happiness to overflowing.

4, 5, 6. *" Behold, that thus shall the man be blessed that feareth the Lord. The Lord shall bless thee out of Zion ; and thou shalt see the good of Jerusalem all the days of thy life. Yea, thou shalt see thy children's children, and peace upon Israel."*

Spiritual blessings shall especially be multiplied. The prosperity of the Church shall be seen, and shall augment the bliss. Converts shall spring up as among the grass, as willows by the watercourses. They shall fly as doves to their windows. Lord grant these blessings, and may our eyes behold the peace of Thy children! So shall we love and praise Thee more and more ! Let us ever bless the Holy Spirit for thus alluring us to Gospel-walk. The picture is enchanting. The real enjoyment exceeds description.

LXXXV.

PSALM CXXIX.

INCESSANT were the troubles of Israel. But they destroyed them not. A prophetic voice here sounds, foretelling evil's final woe.

1, 2. *"Many a time have they afflicted me from my youth, may Israel now say: Many a time have they afflicted me from my youth; yet they have not prevailed against me."*

The burning bush is a fit type of God's servants in this evil world. The flames encompassed every branch and leaf, but still the verdure bloomed. The devouring element was powerless to reduce to ashes. Thus the Church is in constant peril, but still it lives beauteous in freshness and in unfading vigour. Each page of its history recites fearful attacks, but still the inward life survives and no decay appears. The story of each individual believer is similarly the record of trials, troubles, persecutions, and distresses. But still the raging billows engulf not the little bark. It maintains its course. It finally reaches the peaceful haven.

3. *"The plowers plowed upon my back; they made long their furrows."*

This image shows the cruel malice of relentless foes. As the plough urged by much strength deeply penetrates the clod, so scourges and vindictive blows have

mangled suffering saints. We here especially see the
suffering Jesus. Hear His piteous cry. I gave My
back to the smiters and My cheeks to them that
plucked off the hair. See His afflicted form. His
visage was so marred more than any man, and His form
more than the sons of men. While we behold, let adoration swell more warmly, for by His stripes we are
healed.

4. " *The Lord is righteous: He hath cut asunder the
cords of the wicked."*

Vain are the cruelties of the wicked. Their shackles
cannot detain. The Lord wills deliverance. The
chains are broken, and His people are free. So Jesus
was bound in vain. He rises conqueror over Satan and
the grave. He mounts victorious to the courts of
heaven.

5, 6, 7, 8. " *Let them all be confounded and turned back
that hate Zion. Let them be as the grass upon the house-
tops, which withereth afore it groweth up. Wherewith
the mower filleth not his hand, nor he that bindeth sheaves
his bosom. Neither do they which go by say, The blessing
of the Lord be upon you: we bless you in the name of the
Lord."*

A graphic image shows the worthless and ignomi-
nious state of the wicked. Grass on the dry house-top
has no root. It appears only to wither. No mower
gathers it. No reaper adds it to his sheaves. It yields
no good. So the wicked are seen only to be scorned.
Soon they pass away. No benefit results from them.
No blessing cheers them. Shall we have portion with
them ! Forbid it, gracious Lord. We receive Thee as
all our hope and our salvation.

LXXXVI.

PSALM CXXX.

THE essence of the Gospel pervades this hymn. Sin is seen in its odious character. Its due penalties are acknowledged. But forgiveness is proclaimed as leading to reverential sense of God's holiness. The soul waits for the Lord, who is rich in mercy and redeeming love, and ready to blot out every iniquity.

1, 2. *" Out of the depths have I cried unto Thee, O Lord. Lord, hear my voice ; let Thine ears be attentive to the voice of my supplications."*

The speaker cries in deep sense of sin. Convinced by the Spirit of the appalling evil, he lies in the lowest depths of misery. All the billows of wrath seem to be passing over him. There is no shadow of help but in God. With earnest cries he lifts up the supplicating voice.

3. *" If Thou, Lord, shouldest mark iniquities, O Lord, who shall stand ? "*

Confession is made of utter ruin. Our natural state is a mass of evil. Thus in ourselves we stand justly exposed to all wrath. Let us continually pray, Enter not into judgment with thy servant, O Lord, for in Thy sight shall no man living be justified.

4. *" But there is forgiveness with Thee, that Thou mayest be feared."*

The mercy of mercies here shines forth. God appears glorious on redemption's throne. He has provided

forgiveness in the cross of Calvary. Christ's precious
blood washes out every stain of guilt. His righteousness covers all our transgressions. Who will not love
and bless God! They who love Him cannot but love
His holy ways, and dread nothing more than to stray
from the Gospel-rule.

5, 6. " *I wait for the Lord, my soul doth wait, and in
His word do I hope. My soul waiteth for the Lord more
than they that watch for the morning; I say, more than
they that watch for the morning.*"

The Lord has promised never to leave or forsake or
forget His people. He will visit them with the plenitude of His loving-kindness. He will bless them with
the multitude of His tender mercies. For these sweet
manifestations the believer continually waits. He looks
out from His watch-tower as one watching for the
morning, who knows that in the appointed time the
welcome rays will illumine the eastern sky.

7, 8. " *Let Israel hope in the Lord: for with the Lord
there is mercy, and with Him is plenteous redemption.
And He shall redeem Israel from all his iniquities.*"

In great mercy we are called to the full assurance,
that our hope in God shall never. be disappointed.
Reality will surpass all expectation. Mercy sits beside
Him on His throne, and ever loves to visit and cheer
the ransomed people. The redemption decreed and
accomplished is a cup which ever overflows. We cannot exhaust it. It is more than sufficient for all our
need. Every sin shall disappear, and we shall be presented before the throne, holy and pure as our Lord is
holy and pure. Happy are they who know the Gospel's
joyful sound!

LXXXVII.

PSALM CXXXI.

THE Psalmist avows his deep humility. Exhortation to hope in God is added.

———————

1, 2. "*Lord, my heart is not haughty, nor mine eyes lofty: neither do I exercise myself in great matters, or in things too high for me. Surely I have behaved and quieted myself, as a child that is weaned of his mother: my soul is even as a weaned child.*"

Humility is a lovely grace. When the Godman trod this earth this was His robe. No ostentation marked His lowly walk. Hear His enchanting words: I am meek and lowly in heart. Hear the Apostle's appeal: I beseech you by the meekness and gentleness of Christ. If Jesus thus trampled upon pride, shall we, poor dust and ashes, lift up haughty heads! Take, too, the example of the noble Paul. Early in his career he professes that he was the least of the Apostles, not worthy to be enrolled in their company. As he grew in grace he deepened in knowledge of unworthiness. He declared that he was less than the least of all saints. Just before he receives the crown of martyrdom we hear his bewailing voice: Sinners, of whom I am chief. If we had like grace, we should similarly despise self. He who is deeply instructed in the treachery and corruption of his own heart, will always esteem others better than

himself. His soul will be deeply conscious of its utter
need. Like a helpless babe it will look for support
from a parent's care.

3. *" Let Israel hope in the Lord from henceforth and
for ever."*

No hope may repose on self, yet all hope is the believer's portion. He can look up to God, whose tender
sympathy feels with our every woe. Let us pray that
our hope may never fail, but daily strengthen more and
more. It will soon end in glorious reality. Israel's
hope will soon be Israel's glory. The lovely prospect
will soon be actual possession. Expectation will be
more than satisfied.

LXXXVIII.

PSALM CXXXII. 1–9.

THE Ark foreshadowed the Church. As such it was the object of pious care. This ode proceeds to enumerate God's promises.

———

1. " *Lord, remember David, and all his afflictions.* "

It is a gracious privilege to be permitted to be God's remembrancers. Faith is encouraged to remind Him of His covenant and of His precious promises. There is, indeed, no forgetfulness with Him. The past, as also the future, is a present page before His eye. But by this exercise we impress on our own minds invaluable lessons. Thus God is implored to bear in mind the story of the suffering David. In him we have a type of the blessed Jesus. Thus the deep import of this prayer awakens God's attention to the expiatory sufferings of the Lamb of God. David was especially a man of sorrows. All believers drink the same cup. The afflictions of Christ's followers are salutary discipline. They wean from the world and quicken the growth of grace. We shall pray God to accomplish His purposes. The furnace of affliction should never be heated in vain.

2, 3, 4, 5. " *How he sware unto the Lord, and vowed unto the mighty God of Jacob; Surely I will not come into the tabernacle of my house, nor go up into my bed; I will not give sleep to mine eyes, or slumber to mine eyelids, until I find out a place for the Lord, an habitation for the mighty God of Jacob.* "

The especial object of this prayer is that David's zeal for the Ark should not be forgotten. Deep and fervent was this zeal. It was the constant inmate of his heart. He longed to conduct the Ark to its resting-place in Zion. He cast away all thought of rest and quiet until success should crown his efforts. We should learn hence that zeal for the prosperity of God's Church should be foremost among our desires. For this we should incessantly toil. For this we should regard all sacrifices as light. Can we truly say, each one, The zeal of Thine house hath eaten me up!

6. " *Lo, we heard of it at Ephratah; we found it in the fields of the wood.*"

The Church is often in depressed condition. The Ark was carried into the Philistines' country, and after its return, it remained obscure and unnoticed. At Bethlehem David could only gather some reports concerning it. At last he found it in the fields of Kirjath-jearim. The Church can never long be hid. The sun reappears after a short eclipse.

7, 8, 9. "*We will go into His tabernacles; we will worship at His footstool. Arise, O Lord, into Thy rest; Thou, and the ark of Thy strength. Let Thy priests be clothed with righteousness; and let Thy saints shout for joy.*"

It is the joy of joys to join the company of true worshippers. Prayer should be earnest that God would manifest Himself in His sanctuary and cause His presence to diffuse hallowed delight. Especially should we pray that His ministers be conspicuous for holiness and pre-eminent as men of God. Then exuberant gladness will fill God's courts with praise.

LXXXIX.

PSALM CXXXII. 10–18.

10. "*For Thy servant David's sake turn not away the face of Thine anointed.*"

The idea is not a vain fancy that Solomon, now established as Israel's anointed king, thus prayed. He beseeches God not to forget the promises to David. In faith of their performance the youthful king is encouraged to persevere in prayer. Let us hence gather cheering support. Believers may thus personally supplicate. By the Spirit's unction they are priests unto God. They may implore, for the sake of the true David, that they may be welcomed at the mercy-seat. May we persist in prayer, looking upwards in the name of Jesus!

11, 12, 13, 14. "*The Lord hath sworn in truth unto David; He will not turn from it; of the fruit of thy body will I set upon Thy throne. If thy children will keep My covenant and My testimony that I shall teach them, their children shall also sit upon Thy throne for evermore. For the Lord hath chosen Zion; He hath desired it for His habitation. This is my rest for ever: here will I dwell; for I have desired it.*"

Remembrance is called to a notable prediction. The throne of David descends in unbroken line to his off-spring. The suppliant pleads for its fulfilment with undoubting faith. It is precious thus to grasp the promises of God. God chose Zion as a type of His Church. He gives assurance that He will maintain for ever the seed of grace. We may rejoice that this

God is our God for ever and ever. He will uphold His people to the end. He will rest in His love. He will make the Church the abode of His continual presence.

15, 16. " *I will abundantly bless her provision: I will satisfy her poor with bread. I will also clothe her priests with salvation; and her saints shall shout aloud for joy.*"

Glorious promises enrich the treasures of the Church. No good thing shall be withheld. All mercies shall abound. Her faithful ministers shall shine brightly in the robes of salvation. Her true servants shall testify their joy with exuberant thanksgiving. Can we give sufficient thanks if we have been called to fellowship with this blessed company!

17, 18. " *There will I make the horn of David to bud: I have ordained a lamp for Mine anointed. His enemies will I clothe with shame: but upon himself shall his crown flourish.*"

The power of the Lord shall be displayed in the perpetual preservation of the Church. It shall be armed with might as the strongest animals are endued with power. Heavenly rays shall be its unfading lamp. While shame will bring contempt upon their enemies, the crown of glory shall rest on the true sons of David. May we study these abundant promises! May we embrace them with thanksgiving! May we live undoubtingly relying on their fulfilment! May we lift up the head as faithful citizens of Zion!

XC.

PSALM CXXXIII.

THE blessings of peace and concord are commended.
May they be sought and enjoyed by us!

———————

1, 2, 3. *" Behold, how good and how pleasant it is for
brethren to dwell together in unity ! It is like the precious
ointment upon the head, that ran down upon the beard,
even Aaron's beard; that went down to the skirts of his
garments; as the dew of Hermon, and as the dew that
descended upon the mountains of Zion: for there the Lord
commanded the blessing, even life for evermore."*
Countless blessings gladden and enrich the pilgrims
whose feet happily climb the hill of life. True joy is
the companion of close walk with God. These pilgrims
are dressed in a lovely robe. Their garment is love
of the brethren in the faith. This is the evidence of
real union with Christ. This grace was the admiration
of the heathen of old. It was the well-known testimony, See how these Christians love one another. This
precious hymn exhibits this union as good, and pleasant, and fragrant, and fertilizing. It is good, as it is in
accordance with the character of our Heavenly Father,
of Whom it is sublimely said, God is love. It is good,
as they who exhibit it show the lineaments and features
of the first-born among many brethren. It is pleasant.
What can be more charming than to see the smile of

love, to listen to the words of love, and to feel assurance that we are encircled by those whose hearts are knit with ours! It is fragrant, for it sheds around the perfume of true happiness. Ointment poured forth cannot refresh the home more than the constant sweetness of harmonious feeling. It is fertilizing as leading to the growth of grace, and as uniting hearts in every holy word and work. Thus it is figured by the holy oil which, poured upon the head of Aaron, ran in fragrant streams to the lowest portion of the priestly robes. It is fruitful as the dew which moistened the summits of Hermon and softened the heights of Zion's range. Let us seek this grace, so blessed in itself, so blessed to all with whom there is intercourse. But this unity implies not tolerance of error. Two cannot walk together except they are agreed. Light can have no fellowship with darkness. They who thus walk together must first have met in Christ. Oneness with Him is the only true bond of union.

XCI.

PSALM CXXXIV.

THE ministers of the sanctuary are exhorted to bless the Lord. In response blessings are invoked on the speaker.

1, 2. *" Behold, bless ye the Lord, all ye servants of the Lord, which by night stand in the house of the Lord. Lift up your hands in the sanctuary, and bless the Lord."*

Public worship is a perpetual ordinance. From age to age God's faithful servants will frequent His house and join in common prayer and praise. It will be their delight meekly to listen to the proclamation of His truth. They who lead in the outward form should precede, too, in inward grace. They who conduct the hymns of praise should be foremost in offering heartfelt thanksgivings. In the early Church the lighted sanctuary was not a silent place during the hours of night. We have a sweet emblem here of the white-robed congregation, from whose lips unceasing hallelujahs sound. May we soon join the hallowed service!

3. *" The Lord, that made heaven and earth, bless thee out of Zion."*

The ministers of the sanctuary are supposed to give response. The grateful reply is, May He, whom we are thus exhorted to bless, pour blessings upon thee. How vast must be the blessings which descend from Him

who is the omnipotent Creator of the universe. In-
finity is the measure of His goodness. All mercies surely
come in accordance with His heavenly decree.   But it
is from Zion that His blessings go forth.   Zion typifies
the Church of which the blessed Jesus is the High
Priest.   In Him God blesses His people with all blessings in heavenly places.   He that spared not His own
Son, but delivered Him up for us all, how shall He not
with Him also freely give us all things.   Heavenly
Father, we bless Thee for Jesus ; evermore bless us in
Him !

XCII.

PSALM CXXXV. 1—9.

EXHORTATIONS to praise the Lord are reiterated. Motives to this exercise are boundless, and are piously set forth.

— ————————

1, 2, 3. *" Praise ye the Lord. Praise ye the name of the Lord; praise Him, O ye servants of the Lord. Ye that stand in the house of the Lord, in the courts of the house of our God, praise the Lord ; for the Lord is good; sing praises unto His name; for it is pleasant."*

Fervour never should relax in awakening others to give praise. Every faculty should burn in efforts to promote this duty. Let ministering servants lead the van and wave the standard. It is most true that no praises can adequately extol God's goodness. Think of His mercies and overflowing love. The infinitude of His love is shown in the gift of His dear Son to accomplish salvation, to endure our curse, to bring us safely to the heaven of heavens, to present us faultless before the presence of His glory. Can we reflect on such grace and not exclaim, The Lord is good! This exercise of praise fills the soul with exquisite delight. It is the joy of joys. It is the antepast of heaven. Let us then call upon all that is within us and around us to bless His holy name.

4. "*For the Lord hath chosen Jacob unto Himself, and Israel for His peculiar treasure.*"

No height of praise can measure the wondrous grace of God in setting His love on sinful sons of men. Everything in them is calculated to excite alienation. Justice, holiness, and truth seem terribly to frown. Still He loves. The gift of Jesus for them is the main evidence. In this love He regards them as His peculiar treasure. He honours them as the riches of His kingdom, as the brightest jewels in His crown.

5, 6. "*For I know that the Lord is great, and that our Lord is above all gods. Whatsoever the Lord pleased, that did He in heaven, and in earth, in the seas, and all deep places.*"

We cannot too often ponder the almightiness of God. Every view awakens admiration. The gods of the heathen are vanity, and less than dust and chaff. His will is power in the highest. His decrees prevail in every part of His dominions, in all the earth, in all above it, in all beneath it. His power rules unlimited and supreme.

7. "*He causeth the vapours to ascend from the ends of the earth: He maketh lightnings for the rain: He bringeth the wind out of His treasuries.*"

The wild elements seem to unenlightened observation to act capriciously and without control. But His power holds them fast bound in His hands. No vapours arise, no lightning flashes, no rain descends, no wind blows furiously, but in accordance with His sovereign will. Let us bless God for His unbounded rule.

8, 9. "*Who smote the first-born of Egypt, both of man and beast. Who sent tokens and wonders into the*" *midst of thee, O Egypt, upon Pharaoh, and upon all his servants."*

Memory should review the manifestations of His power, when with mighty arm He rescued His people from the iron furnace of Egypt. Then wailing filled every house, for the first-born was stretched among the dead. Then terrible plagues swept the whole land with the besom of destruction. O God, who will not reverence Thy glorious power!

XCIII.

PSALM CXXXV. 10–21.

10, 11, 12. "*Who smote great nations, and slew mighty kings; Sihon king of the Amorites, and Og king of Bashan, and all the kingdoms of Canaan; and gave their land for an heritage, an heritage unto Israel His people.*"

He who rescued His children from Egypt left them not in the perils of the wilderness. Many foes confronted them, but their heavenly Lord raised them above all perils. Mighty potentates with powerful armies opposed their progress, but resistance opposed in vain. The victorious host marched in triumph into the promised land. But they entered not without a struggle. The kings of Canaan mustered all their forces to repel the invaders. But they vanished as the chaff of the summer threshing-floor. The whole land fell prostrate before their feet. In this sustaining and enabling help we have a precious picture of God's unfailing care of His people. He who begins a good work in them performs it unto the end. They are kept by the power of God through faith unto eternal life. He never leaves them nor forsakes them until they sit as conquerors on their thrones of glory. Let us bless God for His converting grace. Let us bless Him not less for His guardian arm and for His ever-watchful aid.

13, 14. "*Thy name, O Lord, endureth for ever; and Thy memorial, O Lord, throughout all generations. For the Lord will judge His people, and He will repent Himself concerning His servants.*"

From everlasting to everlasting the name of the Lord shall be magnified. His wondrous works shall be the theme of never-ending praise. He will never fail to vindicate His people. If for a little season He may seem to be regardless of their trials, the purport is to strengthen their grace. In due time it shall be apparent that His love failed not.

15, 16, 17, 18. " *The idols of the heathen are silver and gold, the work of men's hands. They have mouths, but they speak not ; eyes have they, but they see not ; they have ears, but they hear not ; neither is there any breath in their mouths. They that make them are like unto them : so is every one that trusteth in them.*"

Marvellous is the infatuation of those who form material images and call them gods. Alas! multitudes as senseless as these idols still throng the benighted regions of this earth. Shall we remit our efforts to send to them the knowledge of the true and only God, and Jesus Christ whom He has sent ?

19, 20, 21. " *Bless the Lord, O house of Israel : bless the Lord, O house of Aaron : bless the Lord, O house of Levi : ye that fear the Lord, bless the Lord. Blessed be the Lord out of Zion, which dwelleth at Jerusalem. Praise ye the Lord.*"

Blessings should ever sound from the lips of the ministers of His truth. His faithful servants should re-echo His praise. Who should bless Him more than ourselves ? Let us loudly shout and never end our grateful hallelujahs.

XCIV.

PSALM CXXXVI.

THE mercy of the Lord is largely illustrated, and due praises are invoked.

1, 2, 3. "*O give thanks unto the Lord ; for He is good : for His mercy endureth for ever. O give thanks unto the God of gods : for His mercy endureth for ever. O give thanks to the Lord of Lords : for His mercy endureth for ever.*"

In every name, under every title, in every attribute let our God be magnified, honoured, glorified ; and let the constant chorus exalt His ever-enduring mercy.

4, 5, 6, 7, 8, 9. "*To Him who alone doeth great wonders : for His mercy endureth for ever. To Him that by wisdom made the heavens : for His mercy endureth for ever. To Him that stretched out the earth above the waters : for His mercy endureth for ever. To Him that made great lights : for His mercy endureth for ever. The sun to rule by day : for His mercy endureth for ever. The moon and stars to rule by night : for His mercy endureth for ever.*"

His works of creation excite incessant praise. Infinite wisdom orders the whole plan. Behold the earth with all its wonders rearing its head above the waters. Behold the firmament glorious by day, by night studded with lovely orbs. Surely every object bids the chorus to magnify ever-enduring mercy.

10, 11, 12, 13, 14, 15, 16. " *To Him that smote Egypt in their firstborn : for His mercy endureth for ever. And brought out Israel from among them : for His mercy endureth for ever. With a strong hand, and with a stretched-out arm : for His mercy endureth for ever. To Him which divided the Red Sea into parts : for His mercy endureth for ever. And made Israel to pass through the midst of it : for His mercy endureth for ever. But overthrew Pharaoh and his host in the Red Sea : for His mercy endureth for ever. To Him which led His people through the wilderness : for His mercy endureth for ever.*"

Review again His terrific judgments in Egypt. The firstborn lie dead, and mighty deliverance rescues His chosen people. The sea divides to present a dry path. Pharaoh is overwhelmed. Every incident in the story awakens again a tribute to ever-enduring mercy.

17, 18, 19, 20, 21, 22. " *To Him which smote great kings : for His mercy endureth for ever. And slew famous kings : for His mercy endureth for ever. Sihon king of the Amorites : for His mercy endureth for ever. And Og the king of Bashan : for His mercy endureth for ever. And gave their land for an heritage : for His mercy endureth for ever. Even an heritage unto Israel His servant : for His mercy endureth for ever.*"

Mark the victorious march of the beloved people. Mighty kings resist in vain. They lick the dust and perish. Their fair borders become the abode of the victorious host. Again every circumstance prompts the acknowledgment that His mercy endureth for ever.

23, 24, 25, 26. " *Who remembered us in our low estate : for His mercy endureth for ever ; and hath*

*redeemed us from our enemies: for His mercy endureth
for ever.   Who giveth food to all flesh: for His mercy endureth for ever.   O give thanks unto the God of heaven:
for His mercy endureth for ever."*

But the signal mercies vouchsafed unto ourselves
especially awaken this chorus. Redemption is ours from
all our enemies.   Glory is ours for ever and ever.   Who
will not shout aloud, We give thanks unto Thee, O
God of heaven ; we gratefully acknowledge, Thy mercy
endureth for ever !

XCV.

PSALM CXXXVII.

A PLAINTIVE ode bewails the misery of the captive Jews. Their devotion to their country is avowed. Woe on their enemies is called down in language of prediction.

---

1. *" By the rivers of Babylon, there we sat down ; yea, we wept, when we remembered Zion."*

A pensive group is pictured. We see the mourning captives seated by the banks of the waters of Babylon. Fast flowing tears betoken the anguish of their wounded hearts. Whence comes this piteous grief ? They are removed from their beloved Zion. Their thoughts uncaptured wander through their early haunts. Can reflection fail to weep ? Hard are the hearts which mourn not when parted from their native land and the loved ordinances of God's house.

2. *" We hanged our harps upon the willows in the midst thereof."*

The harps once used in public service, and as the solace of their homes, now bring no joy. Their sight awakens pangs of regret. Therefore they hang untouched upon the neighbouring trees.

3. *" For there they that carried us away captive required of us a song ; and they that wasted us required of us mirth, saying, Sing us one of the songs of Zion."*

Their insulting captors mocked their misery. In derision they bade them tune again their harps, and for amusement to sing as in the happy days of Zion. Tender feeling is a stranger to the hearts of the enemies of God.

4. " *How shall we sing the Lord's song in a strange land ?*"

A sad response checks the taunting wish. The pensive captives reply that no melody could proceed from them. They are far distant from their much-loved Zion; and sounds of woe can be their only utterance.

5, 6. " *If I forget Thee, O Jerusalem, let my right hand forget her cunning. If I do not remember Thee, let my tongue cleave to the roof of my mouth ; if I prefer not Jerusalem above my chief joy.*"

The claims of Jerusalem on the warmest affections are forcibly expressed. It is desired that all intelligence may decline, if Jerusalem ever ceased to be the much-loved object of the heart. Forgetfulness of skill and silent lips should be the lot of those who could prefer any happiness to that of thought of Jerusalem. We should, indeed, rank as unworthy of any blessing, if ever we failed to exalt Thee, O blessed Jesus, as chief among ten thousand and altogether lovely.

7, 8, 9. " *Remember, O Lord, the children of Edom in the day of Jerusalem ; who said, Rase it, rase it, even to the foundation thereof.   O daughter of Babylon, who art to be destroyed ; happy shall he be, that rewardeth thee as thou hast served us.   Happy shall he be, that taketh and dasheth thy little ones against the stones.*"

If the final issue be brought into view, it will be seen

how happy are the captives as contrasted with their sub-
jugators. The former suffer anguish for a brief period,
the latter are doomed to everlasting destruction. Let
us bless God that shelter is provided in Christ Jesus
from the indignation and wrath ready to fall on mystic
Babylon.

XCVI.

PSALM CXXXVIII.

PRAISE is vowed unto the Lord. This debt should
be devoutly paid. The Lord is worthy to be trusted.

1, 2. *"I will praise Thee with my whole heart; before
the gods will I sing praise unto Thee. I will worship
toward Thy holy temple, and praise Thy name for Thy
loving-kindness, and for Thy truth: for Thou hast
magnified Thy word above all Thy name."*

No joy can surpass the delight of thanksgiving. It
is a thrice blessed exercise. It brings down heaven
into the heart. It should engage all the affection of the
inner man. Cold praise is an insulting mockery. No
fear of man should check this utterance. Before earth's
highest potentates timidity should not bring silence.
But especially should we take pleasure in the praises
of holy ordinances. God's love and truth should
have the loudest notes. His faithful performance of His precious promises demand acknowledgment. There is no brighter jewel in the crown of His
attributes.

3. *" In the day when I cried Thou answeredst me, and
strengthenedst me with strength in my soul."*

Experience is a grand encouragement in holy
duties. The soul is lively and hopeful, when it can
point to promises all fully redeemed. It is delight to

know that when in Christ's name we seek spiritual strength we offer petitions which will surely have response, because in accordance with God's mind.

4, 5. "*All the kings of the earth shall praise Thee, O Lord, when they hear the words of Thy mouth. Yea, they shall sing in the ways of the Lord : for great is the glory of the Lord.*"

The day shall surely come when the kingdoms of this world shall become the kingdoms of the blessed Jesus, and He shall reign for ever and ever. Let us by constant prayer hasten this happy time.

6. "*Though the Lord be high, yet hath He respect unto the lowly : but the proud He knoweth afar off.*"

Our Heavenly Father humbles Himself to behold the things which are in heaven and earth; but His eyes regard the lowly with especial favour. Let us be clothed with humility, thus shall we meeten for robes of glory.

7. "*Though I walk in the midst of trouble, Thou wilt revive me : Thou shalt stretch forth Thine hand against the wrath of mine enemies, and Thy right hand shall save me.*"

In our heavenward course troubles will beset us on the right hand and on the left. But let no fears depress us. The Lord will strengthen and refresh us. He will cause our graces to blossom like the rose. His mighty power shall be manifested in our behalf, and we shall stride victorious over all hindrances.

8. "*The Lord will perfect that which concerneth me: Thy mercy, O Lord, endureth for ever: forsake not the works of Thine own hands.*"

May the Lord give us grace to clasp to our hearts

the truths of this most precious verse! He who has begun the work will surely bring it to perfection. If the foundation be truly laid, the topstone will be brought forth with shouts of, Grace to it, Grace to it! Desertion is unknown in the kingdom of the blessed Jesus.

XCVII.

PSALM CXXXIX. I–I2.

ALL things are naked and open to the omniscience of
God. His presence is all-pervading. Suitable prayer
concludes the hymn.

———————

1, 2, 3, 4, 5. *" O Lord, Thou hast searched me, and
known me. Thou knowest my down-sitting and mine up-
rising : Thou understandest my thought afar off. Thou
compassest my path, and my lying down, and art ac-
quainted with all my ways. For there is not a word in
my tongue, but, lo, O Lord, Thou knowest it altogether.
Thou hast beset me behind and before, and laid Thine
hand upon me."*

God's all-seeing eye and all-pervading presence are
indisputable. His thorough knowledge of all the events
in which we are intermixed, His close reading of
every movement of the inner man, His observation of
the characters, His distinct perception of every thought
and word and deed, of every step taken, of every wish
conceived, are acknowledged truths. Never do we come
in or go out, never do we rise or sit down, but His eye
marks. Our lips never open, no utterance ever sounds,
but His all-hearing ear discerns the purport. A re-
cording book is written. We are always surrounded by
His power, and never can escape His hand.

6. *" Such knowledge is too wonderful for me ; it is high,
I cannot attain unto it."*

This knowledge is quite infinite, and therefore cannot be comprehended by finite mind. We can only ponder, wonder, and adore. But when duly pondered, what comfort springs to the believer. Amid all his countless transgressions, he knows that he desires to walk at each moment in the faith and fear of God, and his constant prayer is, Lord, what wilt Thou have me do? Thus he thinks on God, and peace is his soft pillow.

7, 8, 9, 10, 11, 12. " *Whither shall I go from Thy Spirit? or whither shall I flee from Thy presence? If I ascend up into heaven, Thou art there: if I make my bed in hell, behold, Thou art there. If I take the wings of the morning, and dwell in the uttermost parts of the sea, Even there shall Thy hand lead me, and Thy right hand shall hold me. If I say, Surely the darkness shall cover me; even the night shall be light about me. Yea, the darkness hideth not from Thee; but the night shineth as the day: the darkness and the light are both alike to Thee.*"

No terms can fully describe God's omnipotence. There is no spot in heaven or earth which He fills not. There is no covert which affords concealment. He sits above the highest heavens. He descends below the lowest depths. Alas! the folly of poor blinded man, who deceives himself by hopes that he can elude discovery. His every step is in the clear light of God's countenance. The day is near when all shall be proclaimed. Oh! that the Holy Spirit would write this truth with power on our minds! The thought would operate as a strong warning against sin. The check would constantly operate, how can I do this great wickedness and sin against God?

XCVIII.

PSALM CXXXIX. 13–24.

13, 14, 15, 16. " *For Thou hast possessed my reins:
Thou hast covered me in my mother's womb. I will
praise Thee; for I am fearfully and wonderfully made:
marvellous are Thy works; and that my soul knoweth
right well. My substance was not hid from Thee, when I
was made in secret, and curiously wrought in the lowest
parts of the earth. Thine eyes did see my substance, yet
being unperfect; and in Thy book all my members were
written, which in continuance were fashioned, when as yet
there was none of them."*

God's thorough knowledge of us and all our ways is
patent from His creative power. Before we breathed,
His will arranged our incipient being. What mechan-
ism can be more exquisite in all its parts than the
formation of our bodies! Divine skill is manifested
in the design of its innumerable members. Wonder
is exhausted in the contemplation. Select any part,
it proclaims that infinite wisdom devised the plan,
and infinite power brought it to perfection. Can
this great Creator not have most intimate acquaintance with the beings which He thus formed?

17, 18. " *How precious also are Thy thoughts unto me,
O God! how great is the sum of them! If I should count
them, they are more in number than the sand: when I
awake, I am still with Thee."*

There is much transport in the knowledge that God

thinks on us. If we cannot escape His observant eye, so too we cannot be hid from His vigilant love. He loved His people before their members were framed, and never has His love relaxed. The value of this knowledge is inestimable, even as the multitude of His thoughts exceed enumeration. The child of God delightedly ponders this truth throughout his waking hours. They attend him until he closes his eyes in nightly repose, and when perception again returns, and the mind resumes its exercise, the same truth continues to gladden.

19, 20, 21, 22. "*Surely Thou wilt slay the wicked, O God: depart from me therefore, ye bloody men. For they speak against Thee wickedly, and Thine enemies take Thy name in vain. Do not I hate them, O Lord, that hate Thee? and am not I grieved with those that rise up against Thee? I hate them with perfect hatred; I count them mine enemies.*"

When we remember how great is God's love, and how countless His fatherly thoughts, the mind mournfully turns to those who have no part in this precious portion. Alas! there are many who must be reckoned as haters of God. Terrible, indeed, is their doom. It is denounced, They that would not that I should reign over them bring hither and slay them before Me. If their steps are in the way of destruction, surely we shall refuse to walk with them. Love to God will estrange from all who hate Him.

23, 24. "*Search me, O God, and know my heart; try me, and know my thoughts; and see if there be any wicked way in me, and lead me in the way everlasting.*"

Faith boldly calls upon God thoroughly to investigate the heart, and to search its recesses with the lamp of divine truth. The desire glows, that every detected error may be slain, and that the feet may be guided into the way of eternal life. May this be our constant prayer, and may the issue of our walk through life be the heavenly home and the joys at God's right hand for evermore !

XCIX.

PSALM CXL.

IN times of extreme distress deliverance is sought from
God. He is extolled as the protector of His people.
Faith looks to Him as the destroyer of all adversaries.

———————

1, 2, 3. "*Deliver me, O Lord, from the evil man: preserve me from the violent man; which imagine mischiefs
in their heart: continually are they gathered together for
war.   They have sharpened their tongues like a serpent:
adders' poison is under their lips.*"

Since sin defiled this earth, enmity has existed between the seed of the serpent and the children of the
promised Saviour.   This wickedness has been displayed in every form of outward persecution.   Schemes
of secret malice have been its fruit.   Violent assaults
are made.   Venomous calumnies are circulated.   Unaided strength is vain to escape.   But God is ever near,
ready to protect.   To Him should application be made.
Earnest and incessant prayer should plead.   Fruitless
will be all efforts to destroy, if God in answer arises to
give help.

4, 5. "*Keep me, O Lord, from the hands of the wicked;
preserve me from the violent man, who have purposed to
overthrow my goings.   The proud have hid a snare for
me, and cords: they have spread a net by the way-side;
they have set gins for me.*"

So long as persecution rages heaven must be besieged. The resolve to destroy the godly is not always openly avowed. Frequently traps and gins are set to ensnare unwary feet. This was the experience of David. But the knowledge of these acts was salutary discipline, and led to close intercourse with a prayer-hearing and prayer-answering God.

6. "*I said unto the Lord, Thou art my God: hear the voice of my supplications, O Lord.*"

Blessed, indeed, are the prayerful moments when we can appeal to the Lord that He is our God. Who can conceive all that is contained in the name of God? But all that God is, He is to the happy people. Can we desire more? Happy indeed is our case, if we have the Lord for our God.

7. "*O God the Lord, the strength of my salvation, Thou hast covered my head in the day of battle.*"

What must that salvation be which has omnipotence for its strength! Who can injure those who are thus saved by the Lord. They may be called to fight the good fight of faith. Fiery darts may fly around, but none can inflict mortal wound. God, who is the helmet, must be pierced before the head can be reached.

8, 9, 10, 11, 12, 13. "*Grant not, O Lord, the desires of the wicked: further not his wicked device, lest they exalt themselves. As for the head of those that compass Me about, let the mischief of their own lips cover them. Let burning coals fall upon them: let them be cast into the fire; into deep pits, that they rise not up again. Let not an evil speaker be established in the earth: evil shall hunt the violent man to overthrow him. I know that the Lord will maintain the cause of the afflicted, and the right of the poor.   Surely the righteous shall give thanks unto Thy name ; the upright shall dwell in Thy presence."*

Let peace ever reign in the believer's heart. The Lord on His side will crush His foes. The mischief plotted by them will be the pit which shall overwhelm them. The cause of the afflicted and the right of the poor shall gloriously be established. Dwelling in the constant light of God's smile, the righteous shall give everlasting thanks. Happiness now and for ever is their portion.

C.

PSALM CXLI.

THIS hymn commences with a general prayer for acceptance. It then branches into diverse petitions. Thus it stands a tree of solid stem bearing variety of fruit.

1, 2. *" Lord, I cry unto Thee : make haste unto me ; give ear unto my voice, when I cry unto Thee. Let my prayer be set forth before Thee as incense, and the lifting up of my hands as the evening sacrifice."*

Free access to the throne of grace is an inestimable privilege. No words can duly show the condescension of our God in permitting us to wrestle with Him, and not relax our grasp until responses come. May we delight in roaming in this field! When we draw near in the name of Jesus, heaven is fragrant with the perfume of His merits. Such prayer gains audience. It claims acceptance as the appointed evening service.

3. *" Set a watch, O Lord, before my mouth ; keep the door of my lips."*

That the words of our mouth may be always acceptable in His sight, let us pray that the Spirit may ever guard its portals. No unadvised word will thus escape our lips, or come unwelcome to the bar of heaven.

4. *" Incline not my heart to any evil thing, to practise wicked works with men that work iniquity ; and let me not eat of their dainties."*

There is contagion in surrounding evil. The atmosphere is pestilential. Hence let us pray that our hearts may not be beguiled into evil compliance, or fascinated by the miscalled pleasures of sin. False are the allurements. To be thus captivated is to sip poison's cup.

5. " *Let the righteous smite me, it shall be a kindness; and let him reprove me, it shall be an excellent oil, which shall not break my head: for yet my prayer also shall be in their calamities.*"

Life is happy when we are surrounded with godly friends. Their precious counsels guide from evil. Their pious admonitions are fragrant as balmy-oil. They never inflict a rankling wound. We may claim such kindness when it is our resolve to pray for mercies on our adversaries. Let us know no other revenge.

6. " *When their judges are overthrown in stony places, they shall hear my words; for they are sweet.*"

Calamities to the wicked are portended under a graphic image. This shall be the season of tender expostulation from the righteous, and gentle words should strive to win from evil.

7, 8, 9, 10. " *Our bones are scattered at the grave's mouth, as when one cutteth and cleaveth wood upon the earth. But mine eyes are unto Thee, O God the Lord: in Thee is my trust; leave not my soul destitute. Keep me from the snares which they have laid for me, and the gins of the workers of iniquity. Let the wicked fall into their own nets, whilst that I withal escape.*"

Heartless is the persecutor's rage. They would hew to pieces the followers of the Lord with the indifference of a woodman scattering chips by his axe. But the saints in their utmost distress look to their God, and so obtain comfort and deliverance. Especially they seek guidance to keep them safe from the snares so craftily laid in their path. It is just that they who plot such mischief should themselves be entrapped. With such pleas to present at the mercy-seat, with God so ready to succour, let us fear no evil. Let us fly with eager wings to spread our need before our heavenly Lord.

CI.

PSALM CXLII.

THE Psalmist is beset with trouble on every side.   All refuge failed him but his God.   To God he has instant recourse.

———

1, 2. "*I cried unto the Lord with my voice: with my voice unto the Lord did I make my supplication. I poured out my complaint before Him; I showed before Him my trouble.*"

Troubles will surely meet us in our upward march. Let there be no vain attempt to endure in our own strength.   We are weak to bear the crushing load.   Let us rather bring all to the mercy-seat. Let us cast them at the feet of Him who careth for us.   Who ever looked to heaven and failed to find relief ?   If God vouchsafes His presence, all burdens will be light.

3. "*When my spirit was overwhelmed within me, then Thou knewest my path: in the way wherein I walked have they privily laid a snare for me.*"

When troubles come in like a flood, Omniscience marks our every step.   It is good when we can call God to witness that our true desire is to walk closely by His side.   But the cruel enemy will strive to fill this path with snares.

4, 5. "*I looked on my right hand, and beheld, but there was no man that would know me: refuge failed me ; no man cared for my soul. I cried unto Thee, O Lord: I said, Thou art my refuge and my portion in the land of the living."*

Vain is the help of man. Worldly friends soon vanish when the cause is adverse. Such desertion is grievous aggravation of distress. To this the blessed Jesus was most exposed. They all forsook Him and fled. Such, too, is the common lot of His true disciples. Paul mourned, Know ye not that all that be in Asia are turned away from me. But God is still near, and full of compassion. We can approach His ready smile. We shall ever find in Him a sufficiency which no creatures could supply. Safe are they who can say, Thou art my refuge. Rich are they who can add, Thou art my portion. Let us flee to this fortress. Let us rejoice in this portion. Loneliness dwells not in this clime.

6, 7. "Attend unto my cry; for I am brought very low: deliver me from my persecutors; for they are stronger than I. Bring my soul out of prison, that I may praise Thy name: the righteous shall compass me about; for Thou shalt deal bountifully with me."

There are no depths of fear, which preclude a cry to the throne of God. Mercy hears and flies to give relief. Strong may be the persecutors. They may bring us very low. Strong is the arch-enemy of our salvation, but omnipotence is the attribute of our Deliverer. Let us trust, then, and not be afraid. Often are our souls enthralled by the shackles of unbelief and sin and weakness. God can open every prison-cell, and remove every detaining chain. Grateful lips will then ascribe deliverance entirely to Him. The righteous shall see

God's gracious dealings, and flock to our fellowship.
Good Lord, increase our faith, animate our prayers,
strengthen our every grace, that our glad experience
may set our hand to the acknowledgment that Thou
hast dealt bountifully with us.

CII.

PSALM CXLIII.

THIS hymn commences with a general petition, and then expands into a large field of supplication.

---

1. "*Hear my prayer, O Lord; give ear to my suppli-cations: in Thy faithfulness answer me, and in Thy righteousness.*"

David was pre-eminently a man of prayer. His constant abode was at the mercy-seat. He invokes the aid of those attributes of God which shine most brightly in His crown. Faith brings God and all that God is to render help.

2. "*And enter not into judgment with Thy servant: for in Thy sight shall no man living be justified.*"

The thought of appearing before the tribunal of the law is full of terrors. The law exacts undeviating obedience to the rule of perfect love of God and perfect love to man. A curse is denounced on every transgression. The law allows not the plea of penitence or reformation. It listens not to cries for pardon. Its severe code admits no mitigation. Let us flee to the covenant of grace. There free favour reigns. A Surety appears who pays in His own blood the penalty of our every sin, and robes us in His perfect obedience. Oh! precious Gospel, worthy of the God who gives! Worthy of all men to be received in faith and adoration! May we clasp the glad tidings to our heart of hearts!

3, 4. *"For the enemy hath persecuted my soul; He hath smitten my life down to the ground: He hath made me to dwell in darkness, as those that have been long dead. Therefore is my spirit overwhelmed within me; my heart within me is desolate."*

The cruelty of persecutors cannot soften. David endured distress and sorrow in every shape. He keenly felt the misery, and his heart often mourned in lonely destitution. Jesus trod this path. His followers should advance without a repining sigh.

5. *"I remember the days of old; I meditate on all Thy works; I muse on the work of Thy hands."*

There is sweet consolation in pious meditation. Let this be our chosen pleasure-ground. Let all God's mercies pass before our adoring eyes. Especially let His wondrous exploits in accomplishing salvation for us in the redeeming sufferings of Christ fix our happy gaze.

6, 7. *" I stretch forth my hands unto Thee: my soul thirsteth after Thee, as a thirsty land. Hear me speedily, O Lord; my spirit faileth: hide not Thy face from me, lest I be like unto them that go down into the pit."*

The dry clods gaping for refreshing showers are a picture of the soul athirst for God. It is happy to experience this keen craving, and to spread it before the mercy-seat.

8, 9. *" Cause me to hear Thy loving-kindness in the morning; for in Thee do I trust: cause me to know the way wherein I should walk; for I lift up my soul unto Thee. Deliver me, O Lord, from mine enemies: I flee unto Thee to hide me."*

How precious when morning dawns and perceptive powers are restored to hear the whispers of God's love! Such joy fills the cup of all who trust in Him. How sweet is the assurance that if in faith and prayer we commit our way unto the Lord, He will safely guide us and preserve us from all the cruelty and plots of designing men!

10, 11, 12. "*Teach me to do Thy will; for Thou art my God: Thy Spirit is good; lead me into the land of uprightness. Quicken me, O Lord, for Thy name's sake: for Thy righteousness' sake bring my soul out .of trouble. And of Thy mercy cut off mine enemies, and destroy all them that afflict my soul: for I am Thy servant.*"

Here are important prayers. Let us adopt them as heaven-taught models. Let us faithfully present them. He who gave them will recognize His own voice. Gracious answers will abound.

CIII.

PSALM CXLIV.

BLESSINGS are ascribed to God for great success and victories. Continuance of such mercies is implored. The happiness of God's people is depicted in glowing colours.

1, 2. " *Blessed be the Lord my strength, which teacheth my hands to war, and my fingers to fight. My goodness, and my fortress; my high tower, and my deliverer; my shield, and He in whom I trust; who subdueth my people under me.*"

The royal Psalmist sat undisturbed on the throne. He looked back and surveyed the many conflicts and the hard-won triumphs. He knew that God was the author of all his success. To Him he ascribes the praise and glory. Forms are largely selected from scenes of war. They vividly describe the help and might of God. Whenever we prevail over sin and Satan and temptation, let us remember God, who is all our strength and deliverance. Let us magnify His holy name, with all the energies of our hearts.

3, 4. " *Lord, what is man, that Thou takest knowledge of him! or the son of man, that Thou makest account of him! Man is like to vanity: his days are as a shadow that passeth away.*"

Wondrous is God's condescending love. While we

ponder let us adore. Though we are nothing, and less than nothing, the very vanity of vanities, the shadow of a shade, yet from the high throne of His glory His eye of compassion ever tenderly rests on us.

5, 6, 7, 8. "*Bow Thy heavens, O Lord, and come down: touch the mountains, and they shall smoke. Cast forth lightning, and scatter them: shoot out Thine arrows, and destroy them. Send Thine hand from above; rid me, and deliver me out of great waters, from the hand of strange children; whose mouth speaketh vanity; and their right hand is a right hand of falsehood.*"

To realize God's wondrous goodness is a great encouragement in prayer. Let us take courage and flee to Him in every strait, and seek His aid against all our foes.

9, 10, 11. "*I will sing a new song unto Thee, O God: upon a psaltery, and an instrument of ten strings, will I sing praises unto Thee. It is He that giveth salvation unto kings: who delivereth David His servant from the hurtful sword. Rid me, and deliver me from the hand of strange children, whose mouth speaketh vanity, and their right hand is a right hand of falsehood.*"

The mercies so freely and so largely given should awaken fervent praise. It was so with David; let it be so with us. While he acknowledged that God was all his strength and salvation, he continues to wrestle in entreaties. The more we receive the more we should desire. Let us never cease to encircle the mercy-seat with cries from our adoring souls.

12, 13, 14, 15. "*That our sons may be as plants grown up in their youth; that our daughters may be as cornerstones, polished after the similitude of a palace; that our garners may be full, affording all manner of store ; that our sheep may bring forth thousands and ten thousands in our streets ; that our oxen may be strong to labour ; that there be no breaking in, nor going out ; that there be no complaining in our streets. Happy is that people that is in such a case ; yea, happy is that people whose God is the Lord."*

Prayer will obtain floods upon floods of blessings. The prayerful monarch will reign over a happy, prosperous, glorious people. The subjects will shine in the beauties of holiness, and plenty will superabound in their garners. Let us have confidence that our prayers will call down blessings, and that many will rejoice because we frequent the throne of grace. If there be happiness on earth, it is the happiness of those who live in the service of the God of their salvation.

CIV.

PSALM CXLV.

PRAISE pervades this hymn. God's various claims are duly expounded. May they so influence our hearts that much fruit may ripen!

1, 2. "*I will extol Thee, my God, O King; and I will bless Thy name for ever and ever. Every day will I bless Thee; and I will praise Thy name for ever and ever.*"

Such is the hearty resolve of faith. May it in truth be our very life. Happily will flow the days which are preparation for the home in which praises never ebb.

3. "*Great is the Lord, and greatly to be praised; and His greatness is unsearchable.*"

Who can measure the infinitude of the Lord! But as we praise, the topic will delightfully expand. Eternity will not exhaust it.

4. "*One generation shall praise Thy works to another, and shall declare Thy mighty acts.*"

The praise of God endures with earth's continuance. The Lord's seed shall never be extinct, and the work of praise will be their ever living joy.

5, 6, 7. "*I will speak of the glorious honour of Thy majesty, and of Thy wondrous works. And men shall speak of the might of Thy terrible acts; and I will declare Thy greatness. They shall abundantly utter the memory of Thy great goodness, and shall sing of Thy righteousness.*"

The theme exceeds all utterance. Let all efforts be made to do justice to it; still the greatness, the majesty, the goodness, the righteousness of the Lord, will scarcely be touched in their outlines.

8. "*The Lord is gracious, and full of compassion; slow to anger, and of great mercy.*"

The believer's experience testifies to this precious truth. Where sin abounds, grace much more abounds. Our need and misery awaken constant compassion. If provocations roused just wrath, we should speedily be cast off. Every moment proves that God is rich in forbearing mercy.

9. "*The Lord is good to all; and His tender mercies are over all His works.*"

Surely goodness and mercy follow us each day. All things show His tender love.

10, 11, 12. "*All Thy works shall praise Thee, O Lord; and Thy saints shall bless Thee. They shall speak of the glory of Thy kingdom, and talk of Thy power; to make known to the sons of men His mighty acts, and the glorious majesty of His kingdom.*"

The saints delight in extolling the name of their glorious King. Superabundant is the theme presented by His dominion. His throne is universal empire. His sceptre is unbounded sway.

13. "*Thy kingdom is an everlasting kingdom, and Thy dominion endureth throughout all generations.*"

From everlasting to everlasting He sits upon the throne of unlimited sovereignty. From everlasting to everlasting His praises shall resound.

14. "*The Lord upholdeth all that fall, and raiseth up all those that be bowed down.*"

Let us pursue our heavenward path leaning on our Beloved. When we stumble He will uphold; when we fall He will upraise us.

15, 16, 17, 18. "*The eyes of all wait upon Thee; and Thou givest them their meat in due season. Thou openest Thine hand, and satisfiest the desire of every living thing. The Lord is righteous in all His ways, and holy in all His works. The Lord is nigh unto all them that call upon Him, to all that call upon Him in truth.*"

All sustenance comes from His bountiful goodness. His open hand pours down plenteousness on earth. Holiness is His glorious attribute. Holiness is stamped on all His works. May the impress on our brow be, Holiness to the Lord! Precious is the thought that the ear nearest to us is the ear of our God, ever waiting to hear and to relieve our need.

19, 20, 21. "*He will fulfil the desire of them that fear Him; He also will hear their cry, and will save them. The Lord preserveth all them that love Him: but all the wicked will He destroy. My mouth shall speak the praise of the Lord: and let all flesh bless His holy name for ever and ever.*"

Precious indeed is the promise that the desire of His servants shall be fulfilled. Salvation shall be their heritage. No harm shall injure those that love Him. But the wicked shall be utterly consumed. May the concluding resolve be the inmate of our hearts! Let universal blessings be ascribed to our Heavenly Father in Christ Jesus.

CV.

PSALM CXLVI.

PRAISE is the Psalmist's sweet employ. God's claims to praise are stated. May they attune our hearts to sing the heavenly theme!

1, 2. "*Praise ye the Lord. Praise the Lord, O my soul. While I live will I praise the Lord; I will sing praises unto my God while I have any being.*"

Gratitude demands that praise should be our untiring exercise. Its performance brings delight. Happy are the hours thus consecrated. Thus earth assimilates to heaven, where Halleujahs are the constant sound.

3, 4. "*Put not your trust in princes, nor in the son of man, in whom there is no help. His breath goeth forth, he returneth to his earth; in that very day his thoughts perish.*"

It is a natural tendency to be influenced by external show. Hence it is a common fault to court the favour of the rich and great. We are prone to lean on their support, and to look to them for help. But every man in his best estate is empty worthlessness. The Lord speaks, and thrones crumble. The Lord speaks, and the palace is exchanged for the grave. Tibni dies— Omri reigns. The grandest prince is but dust: and unto dust he must return.

5, 6, 7. "*Happy is he that hath the God of Jacob for his help, whose hope is in the Lord his God: which made*

heaven and earth, the sea, and all that therein is; which
keepeth truth for ever.   Which executeth judgment for the
oppressed ; which giveth food to the hungry."

While men are emptiness, sufficiency abounds in
God.   Happy are they who find safe shelter in His
covering wings.   Think of His boundless power.   The
heavens, the earth, and all therein are the creation of
His will.   Precious is His treasury of promises.   Not
one shall ever fail.   Their payment may be desired at
the mercy-seat, and surely they will be redeemed.
Many foes oppress His servants, but their efforts are
impotent.   The cause of the righteous is vindicated.
None prevail against them.   All their need, too, is
supplied.   They lie down in green pastures; beside
still waters they repose.

8, 9, 10. *" The Lord looseth the prisoners: the Lord*
openeth the eyes of the blind : the Lord raiseth them
that are bowed down: the Lord loveth the righteous.
The Lord preserveth the strangers; He relieveth the
fatherless and widow: but the way of the wicked He
turneth upside down.   The Lord shall reign for ever, even
thy God, O Zion, unto all generations.   Praise ye the
Lord."

Precious lessons are learned from contemplating
God's gracious dealings.   His people are born in the
prison-house of Satan.   God removes the shackles ;
they go forth free.   They are blind by nature.   He
opens their eyes to see all the wonders of redeeming
love.   Heavy burdens often oppress them.   He enables
them to lay aside every weight so as to run with patience
the heavenward road.   He delights to cheer them with
manifestations of His love.   They are strangers and

pilgrims in an enemy's land. He is their constant guardian. In family destitution He brings relief. But just wrath burns fiercely against His adversaries. For ever and for ever God shall reign inhabiting the praises of His people. Bless the Lord, O our souls. Amen.

CVI.

PSALM CXLVII.

EXHORTATIONS call to praise our God. Let our grateful hearts rejoicingly obey.

---

1. *"Praise ye the Lord: for it is good to sing praises
unto our God ; for it is pleasant ; and praise is comely."*

It cannot be too earnestly enforced that praise is our
duty, our joy, and our becoming exercise. Let happy
experience testify this truth.

2, 3. *" The Lord doth build up Jerusalem : He gathereth
together the outcasts of Israel. He healeth the broken in
heart, and bindeth up their wounds."*

He brought the captive Jews from Babylon. Thus
He showed by expressive type that He will not suffer
the enemy to hold the Church in enduring bondage.
Sorrow and mourning may be long their lot, but at His
bidding, joy will bud forth, and every wound be healed.

4. *" He telleth the number of the stars ; He calleth them
all by their names."*

We are thus taught that nothing can surpass His
knowledge. The starry firmament sparkles with innumerable orbs. All are known to Him. So we, our
persons, our matters, are all patent to His omniscient
eye.

5, 6. *" Great is our Lord, and of great power : His
understanding is infinite. The Lord lifteth up the meek :
He casteth the wicked down to the ground."*

In His wisdom He reads every character. He
knows the meek and exalts them. He knows the
wicked and debases them.

*7, 8, 9. " Sing unto the Lord with thanksgiving ; sing
praise upon the harp unto our God : who covereth the
heaven with clouds, who prepareth rain for the earth, who
maketh grass to grow upon the mountains. He giveth to
the beast his food, and to the young ravens which cry."*

We cannot too frequently exhort to praise. The
merciful dealings in nature are a fruitful topic. Behold
the heavens robed in their raiment of clouds, the rain
descending to fertilize the earth, the summits of the hills
clad in verdure, and bless the hand which thus dispenses
plenteousness. Behold the beasts of the forests and
the ravens in their lofty nests. His hand provides
their food. Let then His hand be praised.

*10, 11. " He delighteth not in the strength of the horse ;
He taketh not pleasure in the legs of a man. The Lord
taketh pleasure in them that fear Him, in those that hope
in His mercy."*

The Lord has no delight in animal or bodily strength
of frame. He looks to the inner man, and smiles on
faith and fear. May such graces ever appear in us.

*12, 13. " Praise the Lord, O Jerusalem ; praise thy
God, O Zion. For He hath strengthened the bars of thy
gates ; He hath blessed thy children within thee."*

The Church cannot be too fervent in praise. The
strength of protecting bulwarks, the happiness of the
inhabitants within, all call for grateful adoration.

*14, 15, 16, 17, 18, 19, 20. " He maketh peace in thy
borders, and filleth thee with the finest of the wheat. He
sendeth forth His commandment upon earth : His word*

runneth very swiftly. He giveth snow like wool : He scattereth the hoar-frost like ashes. He casteth forth His ice like morsels : who can stand before His cold ? He sendeth out His word, and melteth them : He causeth His wind to blow, and the waters flow. He showeth His word unto Jacob, His statutes and His judgments unto Israel. He hath not dealt so with any nation : and as for His judgments, they have not known them. Praise ye the Lord."

All blessings come from the bounteous hand of God and merit praise. His will pervades the length and breadth of the earth, ordering all things and enforcing obedience. But the blessing of blessings is His revealed Word. This is now circulated in almost all the languages of the world. We are abundantly favoured with the inestimable boon. Let us gratefully use it, and adore the gracious Giver. Praise ye the Lord.

CVII.

PSALM CXLVIII.

PRAISE to God is invoked because of His glory in all
things, animate and inanimate. Especially His saints
call for adoration.

———————

1, 2. "*Praise ye the Lord.   Praise ye the Lord from
the heavens: praise Him in the heights.   Praise ye Him,
all His angels: praise ye Him, all His hosts.*"

Praise is due not from men only, but from all the
angelic hosts.   There is, however, a solemn difference.
We are slow to this holy exercise, and need the constant
quickening of the Spirit.   They find it their incessant
delight, and praise is their most willing utterance.

3, 4, 5. "*Praise ye Him, sun and moon: praise Him,
all ye stars of light.   Praise Him, ye heavens of heavens,
and ye waters that be above the heavens.   Let them praise
the name of the Lord: for He commanded, and they were
created.*"

Lift up your eyes to the shining firmament.   Mark
the glorious sun, daily proceeding on its brilliant way,
and filling the world with light and beauty.   Behold
the countless stars bespangling the canopy on high.
No vocal sound, indeed, is uttered; but still they have
a voice which calls forth praise to Him who willed
their being.   As they shine they seem to cry, Praise
the Lord who thus created us.

6. " *He hath also stablished them for ever and ever : He hath made a decree which shall not pass.*"

If praise be due for creative powers, so also for sustaining care. If we praise God because of the original birth of the orbs of heaven, let our praise resound while they continue their brightness. The Word that made them cannot be repealed. Thy Word, O God, is settled for ever in heaven.

7, 8, 9, 10. " *Praise the Lord from the earth, ye dragons, and all deeps: Fire and hail ; snow and vapours ; stormy wind fulfilling His word : Mountains, and all hills ; fruitful trees, and all cedars : Beasts, and all cattle ; creeping things, and flying fowl.*"

The earth teems with animated beings, with things, too, that are inanimate. But they all proceed from God. They all subserve His purposes. They all call for His praise. From the monarch of the forest—from the eagle soaring in the skies to the tiniest insect— from the mountain to the vale—one acclamation is evoked, Let the great Creator—let the unfailing Preserver—receive praise.

11, 12, 13. " *Kings of the earth, and all people ; princes, and all judges of the earth : Both young men and maidens ; old men and children : Let them praise the name of the Lord ; for His name alone is excellent : His glory is above the earth and heaven.*"

From the occupier of lofty estates to the inmate of the lowest hut, from the hoary head to the infant in the cradle, let one sound be elicited. All they are, and all they have, is the free gift of God. For all they are and all they have, let praise be given.

14. " *He also exalteth the horn of His people, the praise*

*of all His saints ; even of the children of Israel, a people
near unto Him.   Praise ye the Lord."*

Pre-eminently, praise is due from the saints of the
Lord, whom He hath redeemed by the blood of His
Son, and sanctified by His Spirit.   From their inmost
souls let them shout, " Praise ye the Lord."

CVIII.

PSALM CXLIX.

CONTINUAL is the call to praise our God. May the call never fail to warm our hearts!

————————

1. *" Praise ye the Lord. Sing unto the Lord a new song, and His praise in the congregation of saints."*

They who can become weary of God's praise would find heaven's work a tedious task. Let us praise Him in our closets, in our private hours. Let us praise Him, too, when we frequent the congregation of public worshippers. Thus, when we leave earth, we shall change our place, but not our work.

2, 3. *" Let Israel rejoice in Him that made him : let the children of Zion be joyful in their King. Let them praise His name in the dance : let them sing praises unto Him with the timbrel and harp."*

Can we restrain praises to our God when we remember that He gave us being, and faculties to conceive His goodness and laud His name. Let us remember, too, that as King of kings and Lord of lords He reigns for us, and should reign in us. When this joy swells warmly in our hearts, it will be manifested by all our powers, and throughout all our time.

4. *" For the Lord taketh pleasure in His people : He will beautify the meek with salvation."*

It is the wonder of wonders that the great and glo-

rious God should stoop to regard such creatures as we
are.   But wonder is immeasurably magnified when we
are taught that thoughts of us are pleasure to Him.
Let gratitude constrain our hearts to praise without
measure and without end.   Not only does He take
pleasure in His people, He beautifies the meek with
salvation! Meekness is their lovely characteristic. This
grace proves them to be followers of Him who avows
Himself as meek and lowly in heart.   Beauteous robes
of salvation are prepared for them.   These garments
are heavenly in structure, fit for the Bride, the Lamb's
wife, meet to adorn the palace of our God.

5. " *Let the saints be joyful in glory : let them sing aloud
upon their beds.*"

Abundant cause impels the saints to praise. They
have received grace as foretaste of glory.   Let them
realize this, and let them sing aloud as if their promised
state filled their hearts with foretaste.   Let not the
shades of night entirely suppress this happy exercise.
In the night season, let not praises be wholly silent.
When the earthly tabernacle moulders in the bed of
death, the liberated spirit will sing with full intelligence
and joy.

6, 7, 8, 9. " *Let the high praises of God be in their
mouth, and a two-edged sword in their hand ; To execute
vengeance upon the heathen, and punishments upon the
people ; To bind their kings with chains, and their nobles
with fetters of iron ; To execute upon them the judgment
written : this honour have all His saints. Praise ye the
Lord.*"

Great is the power of the Word when uttered by
praising lips.   It will subdue all the enemies of Christ's

kingdom.   The happy saints shall be assessors in
the judgments denounced.   Grand is their privilege,
joyful their state !   They cannot praise the Lord
enough.   Let us strive to praise Him more and more !
Praise ye the Lord.

CIX.

PSALM CL.

THE Psalms thus close. But praise shall never end. Let praise be the constant ecstasy of all our powers and all our time. Eternity will prolong, but never end the strain.

———

1. *" Praise ye the Lord. Praise God in His sanctu- ary: praise Him in the firmament of His power."*

Exhortation still stirs up praise. Worthy, indeed, is the Lord to be praised throughout the universe. Let His praise be heard in the public service of His house, where His saints assemble to magnify His name. Let it swell in the highest heavens, where angelic hosts and all the redeemed lift up their joyful voices in adoring strains.

2. *" Praise Him for His mighty acts: praise Him according to His excellent greatness."*

Mighty indeed are God's acts in creation, provi- dence, and grace. Creation is a volume replete with wonders. They surpass all power to enumerate. They exceed all admiration. Providence is wonderful in showing His mind in constant operation. But redemption causes love to overflow in wonder. It excites our loudest shouts. To estimate its exceeding preciousness the eternal kingdom must be reached. The innumerable multitude must be joined before we can fully realize that all sin is washed away, and every transgression pardoned, and the law's curse removed, and righteousness divine bestowed as the resplendent robe of heaven. Then will be the joy of knowing that mercy has brought us to the journey's end; that endless rest is reached and endless hallelujahs placed upon the lips. Then shall eternal bliss flow on; then shall the realm of glory shout endlessly the Redeemer's praise.

3, 4, 5. " *Praise Him with the sound of the trumpet : praise Him with the psaltery and harp. Praise Him with the timbrel and dance: praise Him with stringed instruments and organs. Praise Him upon the loud cymbals : praise Him upon the high-sounding cymbals.*"

In the days of Levitical type and shadow, musical instruments of every form and power contributed to swell the melody. Now, when spiritual service takes its enlightening place, let every rational faculty make our hallelujahs sweet and loud. Art may sing and spirituality still live.

6. " *Let every thing that hath breath praise the Lord. Praise ye the Lord.*"

Meet is the grand conclusion of this book of hymns and odes and spiritual songs. Let us obey the just command. Every breath is God's free gift. Let every breath fly upward on the wings of adoration. But all our efforts can scarcely reach the outlines of due praise.

May the Lord inspire us more and more! May we thus meeten to praise Him better when we cast our crowns before His throne. Praise ye the Lord! Amen and Amen.

THE END.